An Introduction to Assessment

Patricia Broadfoot

continuum

Continuum International Publishing Group
The Tower Building   80 Maiden Lane, Suite 704
11 York Road   New York, NY 10038
SE1 7NX

www.continuumbooks.com

© Patricia Broadfoot 2007

Reprinted 2009

British Library Cataloguing-in-Publication Data
A catalogue record for this book is available from the British Library.

ISBN: 0826496954 (paperback)

Library of Congress Cataloging-in-Publication Data
A catalog record for this book is available from the Library of Congress.

Typeset by Fakenham Photosetting Limited, Fakenham, Norfolk
Printed and bound in Great Britain by The Cromwell Press Group, Trowbridge, Wiltshire

An Introduction to Assessment

Also available from Continuum

Assessment, Lyn Overall and Margaret Sangster

Assessment in FE, Andy Armitage

Marking and Assessment, Howard Tanner

Assessment: A Practical Guide for Secondary Teachers, Howard Tanner and Sonia Jones

e-Assessment Handbook, Geoffrey Crisp

Contents

Part One
UNDERSTANDING ASSESSMENT

Introducing Assessment

This is a book about assessment. It is written for those whose daily lives as education professionals require them to engage in various forms of educational assessment. In the last few years educational assessment has become a more and more prominent part of the business of teaching and learning. From the day-to-day activities of students and teachers in classrooms through to national and international arrangements for monitoring standards, educational assessment influences everything we do in our professional lives.

It is therefore vital that we make it 'the faithful servant and not the dominating master' (Mortimore and Mortimore 1984). An essential first step to achieving this is the development of 'assessment literacy' among all those with responsibility for teaching and learning in institutions. Teachers, lecturers and education professionals of all kinds now readily accept that an understanding of the central issues around assessment and an ability to use assessment constructively is a key element of their professional repertoire of skills.

This book has been written to help all those committed to this goal. It provides an introduction to some of the central issues in educational assessment as it affects individuals, institutions and education systems as a whole since although very different in scale, the rationale for educational assessment, its nature and impact are fundamentally the same at all these levels.

The first part of the book provides an understanding of the key terms and ideas which shape the way we think about educational assessment. It also discusses some of the enduring tensions between the various purposes for which we use assessment. Above all it seeks to explain why issues around assessment are of such central importance to the business of education today.

Part Two looks at the role of assessment in society. It explores the origins of educational assessment historically, and the effects of these historical roots on contemporary practice. It discusses some of the current problems with the way we use assessment, and the role that various forms of assessment play in society today. Part Two also considers the increasing pressure for change and development in assessment both in the industrialized world and in less-developed countries. It identifies some of the pressure points and introduces the reader to some of the new approaches to assessment now being used around the world.

Part Three of the book takes us from the level of the individual learner and the classroom to a consideration of assessment as a policy tool. It describes the recent evolution of assessment as a major element in 'the quality agenda' that many governments have been pursuing in recent years and it explores the benefits and dangers of an increasingly assessment-driven society. Particular attention is given to educational indicators and the use of league tables in this respect. Part Three also includes a discussion of yet another manifestation of this agenda – the development of appraisal schemes – particularly in relation to teachers.

In Part Four of the book, we address a very different focus of assessment – the topical and increasingly powerful issue of the role assessment can play in enhancing students' learning, rather than simply measuring it. We look at the emerging evidence concerning the way in which assessment can impact for better or worse on student learning and explore some of the new tools and techniques now being developed with this end in view. Finally, Part Four offers some practical illustrations from a variety of educational settings to show how these new tools can effectively be put into practice.

Part Five – the final part of the book – attempts to provide some principles for good assessment practice in the light of all these considerations as well as some recommendations about desirable future directions.

So, What Is Assessment?

Harlen (1994) defines it as follows: Assessment 'is the process of firstly gathering evidence, and secondly interpreting that evidence in the light of some defined criterion in order to form a judgement'.

Indeed, as Madaus (1992: 5) has argued,

whatever noun you choose, assessment, exhibitions, examinations, portfolios, or just plain test, they all rest on the same basic technology, that is, you enlist a small sample of behaviour from a larger domain of interest, such as algebra or aptitude, to make inferences about the person's probable performance relative to the domain, and on the basis of the inference, you classify, describe, or make decisions about individuals or institutions.

Madaus goes on to argue that there are essentially three generic ways to judge performance. The first is for the candidate to supply a product. The second is for the candidate to perform an act, and the third is for a candidate to select an answer from several options. A moment's thought suggests that this definition also holds true, whether the assessment concerned is that of teachers or schools or university departments or, indeed, whole systems of education.

However, within this broad set of distinctions it is possible to define the ways of gathering evidence in rather more detail. These can involve, at the most informal level, day-to-day observations by teachers in classrooms or supervisors assessing ongoing work in vocational settings. It can involve the production of exemplar pieces of work. It could take the form of teachers' records of particular events which reveal an aspect of learning which has taken place. Both teachers and vocational assessors are likely to keep records of various kinds concerning a learner's strengths and weaknesses and their achievements.

Then there is the panoply of more formal types of organization for data collection, class exercises and tests, standardized tests, external examinations and so on. Recently, more novel ways of collecting data have begun to creep in, such as self-assessment checklists and written statements, portfolios and computer-based testing; as well as conferences between students, teachers and parents, or between students themselves. In Part Four of this book we will look in more detail at some of the strengths and weaknesses of these various approaches.

The Scope of Assessment

In seeking to understand the role that assessment plays in educational activity, it is convenient to divide the discussion in terms of five central questions. The first of these is the most profound, namely:

• Why do we assess?

And, it is in the light of the decision about purpose that we may consider other options:

• Who is to be assessed and who is to do the assessing?
• What is to be assessed?
• When is it to be assessed?, and
• How is the assessment to be undertaken?

Why do we assess?

Many textbooks on assessment provide a list of the purposes of assessment. An early example identified:

- diagnosis of pupils' strengths and weaknesses;
- assessment of the extent to which pupils have benefited from a course of instruction;
- evaluation of the effectiveness of methods of teaching;
- prediction of pupils' future performance;
- placement of pupils in the most beneficial educational situation. (Pidgeon and Yates 1968)

Nearly ten years later, Mackintosh and Hale (1976) identified a similar list which included:

- diagnosis of learners' strengths and weaknesses;
- evaluation of the outcomes of teaching;
- guidance to assist pupils in making decisions about the future;
- prediction of probable future success;
- selection and grading to assign pupils to a particular group.

Yet another list of purposes was provided by the 1988 report of the Task Group on Assessment and Testing for England and Wales – the body which provided the blueprint for the current national assessment system (DES 1988). The four generic purposes of assessment it identified were:

- diagnostic assessment to identify students' learning needs;
- formative assessment to support and encourage learning;
- summative assessment to identify learning outcomes;
- evaluative assessment which is directed at assessing the quality of provision in institutions and in the system as a whole.

Elsewhere, I have suggested a somewhat different, more sociological way of looking at the question of assessment purposes in identifying the four functions of educational assessment as:

- certification of achievement (*competence*)
- selection (*competition*)
- the evaluation of provision (*content*)
- the control of both individual aspirations and systemic functioning (*control*). (Broadfoot 1996)

We shall discuss these various purposes in more detail in subsequent chapters.

> ## Activity 1.1
>
> Which of these various purposes of assessment do you consider to be the most important and why? To what extent might they be in conflict with each other?

Clearly, assessment serves a number of different purposes. Many of the purposes for which assessment is used are based on assumptions about its utility and effect which are rarely questioned. Indeed, a key argument of this book is that we find ourselves today in a society dominated by various forms of assessment, especially in the world of education. Our schools and universities, colleges and training centres are increasingly driven by assessment requirements. Yet, despite the enormous impact of this culture on all our lives, its desirability is rarely questioned, its effects rarely debated. The undoubted convenience of tried and tested assessment procedures underpins a web of assumptions and practices that seems almost inevitable.

This book will explore why this should be, why it matters and what needs to be done to improve the situation. In particular, it will argue that the 'opportunity cost' of many of our current educational assessment practices is profound, both in terms of the impact on the individual and on society more generally.

In the past, it would have been possible to make a broad distinction concerning the overall purpose of assessment between its retrospective role in measuring and reporting *past* learning and achievement as in, for example, exam certificates, and its prospective role in identifying *future* potential and aptitudes when it is used as the basis for selection. However, recently there has developed a great deal of interest among academics and teachers about the ways in which assessment can be used to support the learning process itself. This is often expressed as a distinction between assessment *for*, rather than assessment *of*, learning. It is a development that has considerable significance in terms of how we think about assessment in that it has opened up the spectrum of assessment purposes much more widely and Part Four of this book therefore deals with it in detail.

Central to such considerations is the distinction between 'formative' and 'summative' assessment:

Formative assessment is intended to contribute directly to the learning process through providing feedback which models success and guides future efforts, as well as giving encouragement.

Summative assessment is a point in time measure. It is for 'checking up' or 'summing up' what an individual learner has achieved. It is often associated with reporting, certification and selection.

Elsewhere I have tried to capture the inseparability of curriculum and assessment issues by coining a new word – 'curssessment' (Broadfoot 1989). Ugly as it is, this word may help to emphasize that these two fundamental aspects of education can never really be separated. As has often been said, 'the assessment tail nearly always wags the curriculum dog'! In discussing the purposes of assessment, it is also useful to make a distinction between assessment for *curriculum*, that is assessment which is an integral part of the ongoing teaching and learning process; and assessment for *communication*, which concerns all those aspects of assessment which have to do with providing information for potential users, whether this is about students, teachers, institutions or systems. Although there are many parallels here to the distinction between formative and summative assessment, the distinction between assessment for curriculum and assessment for communication makes more emphatic the fundamental tension between the different roles of educational assessment.

At one extreme of the continuum of assessment purposes is the 'diagnostic discourse' – the private evaluative conversation that both teachers and students engage in their heads as they monitor the learning process on an ongoing basis: 'How am I doing? This is so boring! Will I be finished first?' are some of the thoughts that may typically be going through learners' minds. 'Is she paying attention? He looks unhappy – he may need me to explain this again' are some of the many monitoring observations teachers will make as part of their internal 'diagnostic discourse'.

By contrast, the collection of marks and grades that typically sits in books and on record forms and reports is much more likely to be 'dead data'. It often makes very little contribution to the business of teaching and learning itself where its primary function is reporting progress, accountability and selection (Broadfoot 1996a).

It should already be apparent that there is a fundamental tension between the two broad roles of assessment – for curriculum and for communication. This is a tension that we will return to repeatedly in this book.

Activity 1.2

Consider whether you are clear about the difference between 'assessment for curriculum' and 'assessment for communication'. Can you list some examples?

Who assesses?

This question is closely related, clearly, to the previous one of 'why assess?' The purpose of assessment will dictate who carries it out. The decision will also be influenced by who is paying for the assessment. A moment's thought will serve to highlight the inherent tensions between the purposes that teachers and other professionals might have for assessment as opposed to the candidates themselves, parents, the government and society as a whole. There will be aspects of common ground between these various groups in their shared concern with quality and with the need for fairness, but there will be important differences of emphasis too. For government, for example, the acceptability of the assessment, its perceived legitimacy by the public, is usually paramount. For parents, by contrast, the priority may be that of motivation or minimizing the degree of stress the assessment causes for their children. However, traditionally and still today, most assessment has been conducted by those responsible for teaching, whether this is in schools, in higher education, or in workplace settings, where the assessor is likely to be the worker's supervisor.

More recently, however, two other partners have joined the ranks of the assessors. The first of these is the students themselves who, increasingly, are being called upon to engage in self-assessment and also assessment of each other, as a means of helping them understand their own learning. We explore this development in more detail in Part Four. The other new member of the assessment team is the government. Although school inspectors are a familiar feature of most education systems, in recent years the activities of these individuals have been greatly strengthened by the advent of various new kinds of monitoring device aimed at enhancing both the accountability and the overall performance of the education system. It is the advent of the government as a major source of assessment which is fundamental to the advent of assessment as a key policy tool, and we discuss this in more detail in Part Three.

What is assessed?

Traditionally, most forms of formal student assessment have involved reading and writing – the so-called 'paper and pencil tests'. However, traditional tests and exams cover a very small portion of the potential range of skills, competencies and aptitudes that might usefully be included. As long ago as 1992, an influential report suggested that all the following aspects are potential areas for assessment:

1 written expression, knowledge retention, organization of material, appropriate selection . . .

2 practical, knowledge application, oral, investigative skills . . .

3 personal and social skills, communication and relationships, working in groups, initiative, responsibility, self-reliance, leadership . . .

4 motivation and commitment, perseverance, self-confidence, constructive acceptance of failure . . .
(Hargreaves 1992)

This is an argument that Hargreaves has strongly reiterated in his latest book (Hargreaves 2004: 12) in which he stresses the importance of generic skills such as:

• managing one's own learning
• problem-solving

- thinking
- research, enquiry and investigation
- invention, enterprise and entrepreneurship
- communication
- social and interpersonal
- teamwork
- leadership.

Most important of all, Hargreaves suggests, is the role that assessment plays in supporting the development of 'learning to learn'. A key point here is that 'what is assessed' is not to be confined to the traditional areas of knowledge and understanding – often referred to as 'the cognitive domain'. Not only are skills involved but so also are personal qualities, what is typically termed 'the affective domain'. As we shall see later, assessing these vitally important dimensions poses fundamental challenges to the traditional assessment toolkit and therefore requires a very different set of assumptions and techniques.

Perhaps the most central point to bear in mind in any consideration of what is to be assessed, is the argument made above, namely that the assessment tail tends to wag the curriculum dog. Teachers and students both know very well that what is assessed will be likely to form the priorities for learning, just as governments have recently realized that what is assessed in terms of institutional quality and subsequently translated into the indicators which form the basis of public judgement and league tables, is also likely to be a key driver of institutional priorities. This phenomenon, often called 'the washback effect', is one of the most important, yet least often studied aspects of assessment.

Activity 1.3

Draw up a list of aspects of learning and achievement that might need to be assessed. In considering the list try to identify how each of the aspects you have identified might be assessed and which of them tend to dominate at present. What are the implications of your findings?

When to assess

At first sight this may seem a less important question. However, the issue of when to assess closely reflects the underlying purpose of the assessment. Clearly, teachers' monitoring of students' understanding and engagement is likely to be continuous. If the major purpose of assessment is to encourage better learning, the need for good quality feedback is likely to be frequent.

However, assessment which is more communication- rather than curriculum-oriented, is likely to be more spasmodic and come at the end of a particular unit of learning. This might be, for example, for coursework assessment or school reports. Assessment for certification and/or national monitoring might take place at the end of a key stage of schooling. Assessment for selection is likely to take place when there is the need for a choice to be made, either because there is a requirement to ration among those potentially qualified, and to choose the best of this group; or because such assessment is needed to help students themselves make choices about where to go next.

Where the focus is not student learning but institutional performance, the decision about when to assess is likely to be driven as much by practicalities such as cost and the availability of suitable personnel, as by more educational concerns. School inspections, for example, demanding as they are in terms of preparation and time, are likely not to take place more often than every few years. However, internal self-evaluation for the same purpose, given its more formative character, is likely to be a much more ongoing process.

It should, therefore, be clear that there is a subtle interaction between decisions about what the assessment is for, what is to be assessed and when the assessment should take place, a subtle interaction which is further compounded by the crucial question which has tended to dominate the minds of assessment developers over the years, namely, what form the assessment should take.

How to assess

Reference has already been made to the various forms that evidence for assessment purposes might take. This includes insights gained from informal questioning, from diagnostic tests, from various kinds of observation, self-assessment documents, portfolios and appraisal reports, as well as more conventional teacher assessments and tests and external examinations. If the formal public examination that is so much part of the national currency of assessment represents the most visible expression of assessment activity, it is certainly the tip of a much larger iceberg.

In reality, at virtually every minute of every day, in formal educational institutions, there is a range of different assessment activities taking place, spanning the spectrum from the most informal, at one extreme, to the big set-piece assessment events such as public examinations or school inspections, at the other. These latter, in turn, require a continual cycle of preparation and post-assessment development, as well as the spasmodic experiencing of the assessment itself.

It is this complexity of options in relation to assessment activity that powerfully reinforces the point that there needs to be as much clarity as possible when it comes to making decisions about what to do. In particular, there needs to be a high level of understanding concerning the strengths and weaknesses of particular approaches and, just as important, their likely effects.

Fundamental to any decision regarding 'how to assess' is the issue of purpose, as this will drive the kind of comparison for which the data generated will be used. Perhaps the most familiar type of assessment is *norm-referenced*, in which candidates are compared with one another. This is an approach that is closely associated with competition. Apart from the widespread belief that such competition is motivating for learners, as in, for example, sport, it has also arisen because of the need for assessment that discriminates between individuals where a selection has to be made.

However, a great deal of assessment has always been, and remains, what is called 'criterion-referenced assessment', that is, assessment in relation to a standard. As we shall see in Part Two, some of the earliest forms of assessment were of this kind. In practice, of course, many tests have elements of both. The process of deciding, for example, the appropriate level children ought to achieve in a national curriculum assessment, has been initially identified by some exercise in norm-referencing, although the assessment itself will be criterion-referenced. Driving tests are often cited as the classic example of a criterion-referenced test since they lay down the competencies an individual needs to demonstrate if they are to be allowed a driving licence. However, here again, the decision about what constitutes competence has, at some point, been made on a more norm-referenced basis.

The key distinction here is that, where the emphasis is on criterion-referenced assessment, the goal is that the assessed, whether this is an individual student, a group of students, a teacher or an institution, should be capable of being successful and that all those who do meet this defined standard should pass the test. In contrast, a norm-referenced test is almost inevitably associated with a number of candidates failing, in that it distributes those being assessed in terms of the best to the worst.

Activity 1.4

Table 1.1 summarizes some of the key differences between these approaches. Draw up a list of examples of when the use of one or other of these approaches might be most appropriate.

More recently, a third basis for comparing performance has become widely recognized. This is so-called *ipsative* assessment in which the standard for comparison is that of the individual learner with themselves. Here the concern is to identify an individual learner's progress in relation to their own previous performance. Ipsative assessment is an approach that is, of course, just as relevant for institutions and systems as it is for individuals. It is closely associated with the more recent development of interest in assessment for learning as part of the overall concern with formative assessment.

Two other crucial concepts are needed in the toolbox of the assessor when thinking about 'how to assess'. These are the concepts of *reliability* and *validity*. These terms are now very widely used and have become a familiar part of professional vocabulary. Reliability simply relates to the *dependability* of an assessment. It reflects the degree of confidence that if a different test was to be used or a student was to be retested on some future occasion, the result would be broadly similar.

Validity, on the other hand, concerns the degree to which an assessment is a faithful representation of what it purports to be assessing. There are several ways of looking at validity. *Face validity* refers to whether the assessment being used is convincing in terms of its content as a test of the skill or knowledge in question. *Construct validity* is, by contrast, a more technical term that refers to the extent to which the assessment represents the underlying knowledge or skill that it is intended to.

Validity has been a particular problem in relation to the tradition of standardized multiple-choice testing which is particularly powerful in the United States. This is because such tests cannot easily represent a real-life performance situation. As a result there is now a powerful trend in the United States and elsewhere towards more teacher assessment in the pursuit of more 'authentic evidence' of student achievement through more 'performance-based' assessment. It is increasingly being recognized that a great deal of important information about student competencies has not, in the past, been captured because of the limitations of so-called 'objective' tests.

There is still widespread concern among many educationists that some of the most crucial curriculum objectives such as creativity, are also some of the most difficult to assess in a systematic and, hence, reliable way. Unfortunately, efforts to introduce more complex and authentic tasks which are capable of capturing some of these more ephemeral learning objectives, have often been bedevilled by the almost inevitably low levels of reliability.

One famous example in this respect was the effort of the British government to introduce national assessment for seven-year-olds in England at the end of Key Stage 1 (6–7 year-olds) in the early 1990s. The tasks that were designed for this purpose were modelled on earlier national monitoring approaches involving the testing of a small sample of students. However, what was possible where only a relatively small number of individuals were involved in terms of the elaborate character of some tasks, proved to be impracticable when every child was to be tested. Moreover, the vulnerability to teacher intervention of tests based on such complex tasks when the results were significant for a school's reputation, meant there was significant scope for abuse.

Perhaps the most classic illustration of the problems involved in trying to combine high levels of both validity and reliability on a mass scale is the English nineteenth-century 'Payment by Results' system. In Victorian elementary schools, there was a period during which teachers' pay depended on the level of their pupils' results in basic literacy and numeracy as assessed by the school inspector. Needless to say, teachers did all they could, by fair means or foul, to help their pupils get good marks!

As institutional assessment has become increasingly high-profile in recent years, so it has become apparent that where tests are 'high-stakes' in the sense that important consequences follow from them, for either individuals or institutions, it is essential that the tests or other assessment procedures used are defensible. Hence reliability becomes an overriding issue. However, the price of such reliability, and hence defensibility, is often that the tests become very limited in design and focus, with the opportunity for gathering information about a range of potentially much more important learning objectives having to be abandoned. It is certainly the case, as I suggested earlier in this chapter, that the content of 'high-stakes' tests will influence the priorities of both the individuals who are part of the education system – teachers and students – and those of the institutions themselves. Messick (1995), a leading exponent of validity issues, referred to this as 'consequential validity' and came to regard it as perhaps the most important aspect of validity, despite being the least technical.

As we shall see in subsequent chapters of this book, the tension between reliability and validity is one of the most enduring features of contemporary educational assessment as it weaves its way through many of the debates that take place around the questions of why, who, when, what and how.

Summary

In this chapter we have sought to map the various features of educational assessment. We have considered the full span of assessment purposes and techniques ranging from the familiar activities of the classroom at one extreme, to the increasingly pervasive network of monitoring and accountability activities on the other. We have considered what assessment is, namely the collection of evidence and its interpretation in relation to a standard. We have briefly discussed the various purposes for which assessment is used – from its role in understanding the complex processes of learning at one extreme, to that of providing for the ongoing monitoring of quality at the other through, for example, teacher appraisal, institutional inspection and national evaluation.

As we shall explore in Chapter 2, a central reason for educational assessment has traditionally been the introduction of greater equity and meritocracy into educational provision. Educational assessment developed as a mechanism for communicating achievement and for identifying relative merit in terms of an individual's potential capacity to benefit from future educational opportunities. Increasingly, public opinion has come to trust this arbiter of life chances. Assessment enjoys considerable legitimacy as a selection device and thus plays a vital role in countries around the world in managing individual aspirations.

But despite its undoubted importance in this respect, it is necessary to ask whether educational assessment is indeed achieving the aspirations of individuals and society as a whole for a fair and transparent system; to question whether we could find better methods to achieve these ends. And, as assessment becomes increasingly important as a policy tool, we need to ask whether the benefits outweigh the costs. What price are we paying for our increasing obsession with measuring and raising standards? These are questions which will guide the discussion in subsequent chapters of this book.

Activity 1.5

Consider what is good about educational assessment today and what is most wrong with it. How much scope is there for change and what factors constrain this?

Key references

Broadfoot, P. (1996) *Education, Assessment and Society*. Buckingham: Open University Press.
Satterly, D. (1992) *Assessment in Schools*. Oxford: Blackwell.

Useful websites

www.cambridgeassessment.org.uk/research

The website of the University of Cambridge Local Examinations Syndicate (UCLES) provides a range of research reports and information about various forms of assessment. It is one of the largest agencies dedicated to developing and conducting educational assessment in the world. 'Cambridge Assessment' is the brand name of the University of Cambridge Local Examinations Syndicate.

www.ets.org

This website provides access to another of the largest testing agencies in the world. Its work has been hugely influential in assessment development and research for many years. Based in Princeton in the United States, Educational Testing Service (ETS) provides a directory of tests for a variety of age groups and subjects.

Part Two
ASSESSMENT IN ITS SOCIAL CONTEXT

A Bit of History and the Baggage It Has Left Us

2

It is hard for those who are familiar with contemporary systems of education, as practised in virtually every country of the world today, to understand that the pervasive presence of educational assessment is, in fact, a very recent phenomenon. Most of the history of human civilization has been associated with the provision of some kind of education. However, as is readily apparent, most of this education has been in the form of practical training for economic and social life in the particular culture into which an individual is born. It is only over the last century and a half, as mass education systems have developed, that educational assessment has also developed into a highly specialized, professional domain. A domain that crucially, is associated with the power of science to legitimize the decisions it provides for.

The Historical Roots of Assessment: Competence and Competition

Historically, educational assessment has been neither technical, nor a specialized preserve. It has functioned for the most part in the form of non-competitive, criterion-referenced tests of knowledge or skill, set, administered and judged by adults who know the candidate. Most typical in this respect is the tradition of vocational assessment which dates back, in Europe at least, to the medieval period and the successive layers of accreditation that skilled craftsmen could progress through if they aspired to become a master craftsman. The traditional picture in many other countries is very similar (Goldstein and Sutherland 2001).

Most of the early examples of vocational assessment fall into Madaus' first category of generic ways to judge performance, that were identified in Chapter 1, namely they required the candidate to supply a product. Typically, groups of skilled workers would define the standard that had to be demonstrated by those aspiring to join a particular craft guild. Indeed it was these early stages of vocational progression from apprentice to journeyman, and from journeyman to master craftsman, that helped to form the basis of later, more academic examination systems, such as the French Baccalaureate.

In a very real sense, educational assessment has taken over from previous forms of social organization, including feudalism, to produce a new way of structuring social hierarchy. To a greater or lesser extent, individual opportunity is now built, initially at least, on educational achievement. This is because the radical economic changes of the industrial revolution made the expansion of educational provision during the nineteenth century a necessity. It was accompanied, in Europe in particular, by a growing belief in the power of science and a growing commitment to rational forms of social selection. Thus the means chosen for access to opportunity and privilege, which could be won through schooling, had to seem fairer than hitherto and hence to become more rigorous.

The growing need for an acceptable and efficient way of selecting individuals in the context of growing social mobility, was reinforced by a dawning realization among political leaders in the eighteenth and nineteenth centuries, such as Napoleon in France and Frederick the Great of Prussia, that examinations could also provide an excellent way of imposing centralized state control. By controlling the design and content of national certification systems as well as the increasingly important portals to university education and professional accreditation, the state became a more visible presence against more traditional interest groups such as the aristocracy. By the same token, the power of the state to influence the content of the school curriculum was correspondingly increased.

While such developments are particularly striking in traditionally highly centralized countries such as France, they were also very significant in highly decentralized countries such as England, in which the developing apparatus of examinations provided almost the only national currency in an otherwise fragmented system.

Activity 2.1

Consider the ways in which assessment procedures are designed and used on a national basis in a country with which you are familiar. How big a part do they play in helping to reinforce central control of the education system? What do you see as the advantages and disadvantages of such influence?

Enter the Science of Testing

One of the most significant developments of the late nineteenth century which was to provide powerful reinforcement to the developing industry of formal examinations, was the advent of psychometrics – the belief that an individual's innate intellectual ability could be measured. This capacity, which became known as 'intelligence', was assumed by many scholars of the time to be innate, fixed, measurable and capable of prediction. Thus, where more traditional forms of written examination were designed to measure the standard reached or the quality of a particular performance, the burgeoning industry of IQ testing purported to measure an *individual's actual ability to learn*. Steeped as this movement was in the rapidly developing discipline of psychology and the associated panoply of scientific respectability, it became increasingly hard for either the individuals themselves or their teachers to challenge the orthodoxy of the IQ test.

Thus the modern forms of educational assessment, which began to emerge in the mid-nineteenth century, though they had their roots in traditional vocational assessment practices and the desire to maintain standards of quality in various professions, rapidly became heavily overlaid with an emphasis on competition. Increasingly, it was not sufficient simply to *reach* the standard laid down, but in school, at least, to be among the *best*, and hence well-placed for selection to subsequent coveted opportunities.

Perhaps even more important was the growing association of assessment activity with particular concepts of the human mind and notions of 'ability'. These were to become the prime justification for the massive industry of selection devices that has subsequently grown to dominate education around the world.

Activity 2.2

The notion of 'ability' has become deeply entrenched in contemporary educational thinking. What are some of the consequences of this?

The Need for Legitimation

The advent of procedures that could provide an acceptable basis for educational competition is of central importance in understanding the educational assessment that we have today. Equally, it is important to understand that almost by accident, the need for a higher degree of reliability if such competitions were to be acceptable to those involved, required a form of assessment that was capable of being tightly regulated and policed. This need has underpinned the now overwhelming dominance of the formal, unseen, written examination. This particular assessment technology is both relatively easy to use and also robust in terms of its defensibility against criticisms regarding potential bias, examiner favouritism and so on. In short, it is quick, easy, defensible and relatively cheap. Not for nothing were formal, written examinations successfully used in ancient China over many centuries for the intensely competitive selection of senior civil servants.

Figure 2.1 is a picture of Chung-Quei, the Chinese God of Exams. Having been denied first place in the national examinations he had won, he committed suicide and so became 'kuei' – an evil spirit denied reincarnation and condemned to haunt the world (Christie 1968). This story provides us with a salutary reminder of the tragic consequences to which 'high-stakes' examinations can lead. It also provides a figurative representation of the pervasive and baleful influence of examinations in our world today.

Later, of course, refinements of this approach, in the form of multiple-choice, machine-markable, standardized tests, would provide an even cheaper, more convenient and apparently more efficient means for achieving the same end. Such tests also had the virtue of appearing to be even more objective, hence the term used to describe them – 'objective tests' – though in fact it is only the marking that is 'objective'. As we shall see later, the current rapid development of computer-based testing adds a new and important contemporary dimension to such debates.

The Impact on Curriculum

One side-effect of the inevitable emphasis on written assessment in the development of mass examinations, is the impact it has had on the content of teaching and learning. As formal examinations grew in importance, subjects were increasingly squeezed into syllabuses, the content of which could be tested in written answers. Many would argue that it is from this almost unanticipated washback effect of the advent of external examination systems, that the overwhelming domination of the academic in curriculum content has developed. Indeed a recent President of the American Educational Research Association has cited the remark by Ann Lieberman, namely 'that the history of American education is best understood by the fact that E. L. Thorndyke (a leading psychometrician) won and John Dewey (a leading progressive educationist) lost' (Darling-Hammond). Given the overwhelming contemporary dominance of testing in American schools today, it is hard to even imagine what the alternative might have looked like.

Control: Assessment as a Powerful Tool for Policy-Makers

A fourth and final dimension it is important to note in terms of the history of educational assessment, concerns the issue of control. It has already been suggested that the advent of intelligence testing provided hugely powerful, scientific legitimation for allocating opportunity on the basis of tests. Hence educational assessment for many decades has been relied upon to provide for the control of individual disappointment in the face of failure to succeed. Where such failure is deemed to be the result of inborn limitations it is hard to resist the judgements of the test.

Clearly, too, we can see in this historical account, the beginnings of the potential of assessment to provide a major mechanism for legitimating the status quo with all its inherent inequalities of home background and educational opportunity – as a lever to impose the priorities of those in power on society as a whole. The debate that has raged around the fairness or otherwise of IQ tests in relation to ethnicity, gender and social class, provides a good example in this respect (Kincheloe et al. 1996; Sacks 1999). Critics argue that apparently 'culture-free' IQ tests are in fact inherently biased in terms of their content and language against certain sections of society and favour privileged groups.

Even more fundamental arguably, than even the issue of assessment and social justice, is the overwhelming dominance of educational assessment itself; of the way in which the ideas associated with educational assessment have, over many decades, become so familiar that we no longer notice them or challenge them. For 'models of assessment are similar to any educational model. Such models do not merely describe ideas in practices. They actually work to shape the way people think about and practice education' (Freedman 1995: 102). Certainly it is the case that the features of contemporary models of schooling have now become so familiar that it is almost impossible to imagine what education might be like without them.

However, the message of this book is that it is vital that we do begin to make the familiar strange; to question the accepted merits of tests and examinations and other forms of assessment. We need to question them, both in their own terms, as the fairest way of discriminating between individuals and of judging competence, and in terms of missed opportunities to use the same techniques in more educationally constructive ways. We owe this to the children of today and to the citizens of tomorrow.

Thus subsequent sections of this book explore the arguments that underpin the need for change in more detail. We look first at what I have termed elsewhere 'the myth of measurement' – by making reference to the enormous body of evidence that now exists documenting the more or less inevitable inaccuracies of formal tests and examinations. This chapter is a clarion call to all those in society – parents, students, teachers and above all the policy-makers who have the power to effect change – who have been content up to now to accept, largely at face value, the products of a flawed technology. Who, in the face of widespread student distress and even sometimes suicide, as well as clear evidence that the education system is failing many young people unnecessarily, have apparently been content not to question current assessment practices and to demand a search for something better.

Moreover, the need to consider 'fitness for purpose' is now becoming urgent, not just on moral or educational grounds but also out of sheer economic self-interest. Living as we do in a rapidly changing world, it is vital that the education system delivers the skills and dispositions needed to underpin a thriving and dynamic economy that can cope with such changes. Yet, as we shall see in the next chapter, there is increasingly powerful evidence that current assessment approaches are actively inhibiting the necessary shift in educational priorities and practices, an issue we shall explore by looking briefly in Chapter 4 at the impact of current assessment techniques on the contemporary world. We conclude this section of the book with an exploration of the changing context for assessment and some of the green shoots of change that this is producing.

Key references

Freedman, K. (1995) 'Assessment as Therapy: Review symposium'. *Assessment in Education* Volume 2, Number 1, pp. 102–7.

Goldstein, H. and Sutherland, G. (eds) (2001) 'Assessment at the Millennium'. *Assessment in Education* Volume 8, Number 1 (March).

Sacks, P. (1999) *Standardized Minds: The high price of America's testing culture and what we can do to change it.* Cambridge, MA: Perseus Books.

The Myth of Measurement

When we assess things we also change them. This was recognized by Werner Heizenberg, the Nobel prize-winning physicist in the 1950s:

> Because we observe using instruments which we construct; we interpret what we observe using what we already know and describe what we observe using the language we have available, making knowledge is a constructive, interpretive process. The process of using instruments to observe changes the very nature of what is observed. (cited in Johnson 1991)

This is increasingly being recognized in the natural sciences. But if it is true in this domain, how much more is it true in the human domain where emotions and values, aspirations and anxieties, add their hugely significant dimension to the capacity to perform on any given occasion? Given that all kinds of educational measurement are ultimately interpersonal in character – even so-called objective tests have been created by human beings and are sat for by human beings – it is not surprising that a huge volume of research evidence attests to its inevitable inaccuracies.

The Mounting Evidence . . .

As early as 1935, Harthog and Rhodes' classic *An Examination of Examinations* explored the many causes of potential 'error' in examination results. They cited a range of factors including students' nerves and exam stress, differences between markers' interpretations of mark schemes and standards, marker fatigue and differences in the difficulty of questions. Many of these sources of variability, they suggested, would seem to be almost unavoidable. Countless studies since that time have told a similar tale. They have been well-summarized by the American scholar Mary-Lee Smith, 1991, as follows:

- The teacher may not have covered what is tested in the examination.
- The test may be too long for students to concentrate on it.
- Students may guess if the format is a multiple-choice one.
- The test may be incorrectly normed for a given population of students.
- Perhaps one summative grade is offered which conceals substantial differences in the quality of performance in understanding contributory aspects of achievements.
- The test may measure performance on a given day which has no connection with long-term retention by the student.
- Students may be bored and disaffected and not engage to the best of their ability with the test or examination.
- They may find the questions confusing or ambiguous.
- They may not be able to apply their knowledge because of the limitations of handwriting or other mechanical abilities.
- Many achievement tests merely measure endurance or persistence rather than performance.
- Some students who are divergent thinkers may read too much into the test items.
- Some students become frightened and 'freeze up' in the testing situation, especially those who have no self-confidence or some kind of emotional or family disturbance.

Research in the psychology of assessment has consistently demonstrated that:

- small changes in task presentation;
- in response mode;
- in the conditions under which assessment takes place;
- in the relations between assessor and assessed and within students on different occasions;

all have an effect on the performance. This finding has led some psychologists to extend their understanding of learning by changing their focus from the cognitive processes assumed to underlie performance to the study of 'forms of social engagement' in which the performance is situated (Lave and Wenger 1991).

The scale of variability, and hence errors of judgement that can be involved, is well-illustrated by an experiment reported by Black (1993):

> One hundred students were studying a first-year university Physics course. The students took two parallel exam papers covering the same syllabus, containing the same mix of types of questions, set by the same teachers and marked by the same people. Thirteen students failed both papers but significantly, thirteen failed the first and passed the second and thirteen failed the second and passed the first. Thirty-two students had scores that were either 10 per cent more

or 10 per cent less than their score on the other paper and six students had scores that were either 20 per cent more or less than on the other paper.

Not surprisingly, Black sums up the situation as follows:

> The unreliability of exams is a problem well understood by the creators of tests but not by the public at large ... it is very difficult in a written test to get the information on which you can, with confidence, make a decision about the future of a student. (Black 1993)

And long before, in 1977, the German scholar Karlheinz Ingenkamp wrote in similar vein:

> Traditional oral and written school examinations have been shown to be neither objective nor reliable; their validity jeopardized by subjective influence, their predictive power low (p. 14) ... We have not yet been able to produce research findings to refute the suspicion that we are continually selecting the wrong people with the wrong methods. (p. 62)

Even the invention of so-called 'objective' multiple-choice format testing in the USA in 1914, and the later invention of the optical mark reader in 1955, could not overcome some of the more obvious subjectivities in marking. It could not remove the bias inherent in cultural differences between students; nor could it eliminate the effect of the test situation on students' performance. In short, as was suggested in the discussion of validity in the previous chapter, 'the utility of such tests is questionable since not only are they as unlike real life as you can get, they also fail to represent pretty well every other context in which what has been learned can be demonstrated or applied' (Nuttall 1987: 111).

Activity 3.1

Consider how far you agree with this critique of the accuracy and utility of many conventional tests. What arguments might be made in favour of current practice?

Sociological Significance of the Myth

In short then, the continually increasing significance of educational assessment at all levels of the education system may be traced to a belief in the possibility of applying a scientific technology to the measurement of human achievement and even of underlying ability. Yet, it is a central argument of this book that such measures can never be objective since they are inevitably limited by the social nature of the assessment situation and the values and culture which overlay the interpretation of the quality of a given performance. As we have seen, how well an individual performs in any given assessment situation will almost inevitably be affected by a range of influencing factors – emotional, circumstantial, psychological and social. Equally the judgement of their performance – whatever form it takes – by the assessor, will also be influenced by the same range of factors – emotional, circumstantial, psychological and social. Personal values, motives, politics and external pressures for legitimation are just a few of the cocktail of influences that affect all social action and it is important to recognize that educational assessment is no exception in this respect.

What is both surprising and deeply disturbing, is that this fact of life is so rarely articulated or recognized explicitly. Why this is so and what the consequences of the spurious objectivity which surrounds educational assessment have been for the development of modern systems of education are central themes of this book to which successive chapters will return. For the present, it is sufficient for us to recognize that the concept of educational *measurement* is a myth. But it is none the less a very significant myth. Because of its apparently scientific character, it legitimates a whole variety of evaluative practices which, far from being neutral, operate as a powerful structuring force in society.

Sociologically these assessment practices are enormously significant since they lead to considerable social inequality in terms of who gets what in society. Although examinations were introduced to encourage the development of a 'meritocracy' in which ability, rather than breeding, determined occupational success, it is far from clear whether they have significantly improved opportunity for the socially disadvantaged. University recruitment in the UK remains stubbornly middle-class, inequalities in examination achievement at critical stages both reflecting and reinforcing the social advantages of family background and geographic location. A recent comparative study of local authorities in England between those retaining schools that select at age 11 and those which have comprehensive schools revealed:

> a huge gulf between the population mix of pupils as a whole and the mix in LEAs with grammar schools. In the 19 LEAs that retain substantive selection (each typically with 25% of pupils at grammar schools) just 5.8% of all pupils eligible for free school meals attend grammar schools, while 24.6% of all other children within the LEA gain a grammar school place … the disadvantage of poor children applies even to those of the highest ability. Just 32% of those eligible for free school meals in the top three key-stage II groups attend grammar schools compared with 60% of better-off children. Poorer children in selective LEAs are only half as likely to attend a grammar school as other children with the same underlying ability. This pattern is also true of children with special needs, and those for whom English is a second language. (Atkinson and Gregg 2004: 2)

Thus, while selection is ostensibly on academic achievement, students appear to be very differently equipped to benefit from such 'objective' measures of ability.

> Another recent study of secondary school selection – this time the 11+ examination in Northern Ireland which determines the allocation of grammar school places, produced the startling

conclusion that the highest and lowest grades (A and D) were separated by as few as 18 of the total 150 available marks and the standard error of measurement was of the order of 4.75 with the consequence that the candidate ranking system has the potential to misclassify up to two-thirds of the test-taking cohort by as many as three grades. (Gardner and Cowan 2005)

Such findings prompted the then Minister of Education to the Northern Ireland Assembly to state:

Throughout its history, the 11-plus branded most of our children failures when in fact the real failure was, not the children, but the test itself … I want to make it clear to this Assembly, and to the people, that the tests have no place in the future of education here. (McGuinness 2002: 1)

Despite this commitment, the tests will continue to operate until 2008, an all too typical reflection of the difficulty of providing for selection in a way that the public will accept, by any other means. While the 'myth of measurement' endures, it remains both powerful and useful.

However, there are fears that current public pressure for greater transparency in the examination process will eventually erode existing levels of confidence in the examination system; that a 'general recognition' of the true nature and extent of measurement inaccuracy would fatally undermine trust in the system. It is also the case, however, that not to communicate such limitations will eventually lead to an erosion of public confidence as the increasingly heavy burden of expectations placed on the system exacerbate not only the problems of measurement error but more practical ones as well. To the extent that this is true, it underlines the importance of using assessment in a way that is 'fit for purpose', and of a mature and well-informed engagement with the strength and weaknesses of different assessment techniques.

Psychological Significance of the Myth

Significant as these *sociological* issues are, arguably even more significant is the *psychological* effect that the 'myth of measurement', produces since its products – formal examinations – exert a strong influence in defining both the way in which students engage in education and what they perceive to be its rewards. Examinations tend to encourage extrinsic motivation, discourage cooperation between students, to narrow curricular experiences to what can most easily and reliably be assessed and encourage a 'transmission' approach to teaching in which, for example, dictating notes diverts time from more active, discovery-oriented pedagogies. This is one of the most significant consequences of the continued persistence of the myth of measurement. While we continue to believe in the capacity of educational assessment to provide fair and objective judgements about relative merit, this faith seems to blind us to the overwhelming evidence testifying to the inability of current forms of educational assessment properly to fulfil most the purposes for which they are currently used. It should be a double source of chagrin that such beliefs, such misplaced trust, also work simultaneously to blind us to the very significant positive potential of educational assessment and prevent us seeing the purposes for which educational assessment *can and should be used*. In short it is the myth of measurement that has been largely responsible for inhibiting the positive and creative use of assessment – to *promote*, rather than to *measure* learning.

Activity 3.2

Consider the formal examinations in a subject with which you are familiar. Are there more valid ways in which it could be tested? What would be the problems associated with any such change?

Missed Opportunities

This argument may usefully be developed a little further. One of the main effects of contemporary society increasingly being in thrall to the 'myth of measurement' leading to an obsession with summative assessment, has been to marginalize more fundamental discussion concerning educational goals. Means have become elevated into ends. Testing as a solution becomes a continually improved means to carelessly examined ends. Elsewhere, I have referred to this situation in terms of 'dark alleys and blind bends' – the former where there has been both little or no illumination as to the central purpose of the assessment or the meaning of the results; the latter arguing that a great deal of assessment activity has been located on 'blind bends' where a dangerously powerful technology has been employed with little consideration of its consequences (Broadfoot 2005).

In many countries, the overriding policy imperative for education at the present time is to help maintain a competitive economic edge. Thus raising standards has all too often been elevated to become *the central* objective of educational policy. Many educationists have argued that the consequence of this growing obsession with results is an undermining of the fundamental purpose of education. That rather than teaching students to think, to discuss, to develop values and insights, schools which operate in such a policy context are increasingly simply 'teaching the test'.

Shepard, a recent president of the American Educational Research Association, expresses it thus:

> The negative effects of high-stakes testing on teaching and learning are well known. Under intense pressure, testing scores are likely to go up without a corresponding improvement in student learning. In fact, distortions in what and how students are taught may actually decrease students' conceptual understanding. (Shepard 2000: 14)

In England

> in its drive to make education more and more accountable, the Government has squeezed out room for the elements that keep children involved in the process and that allow real education to take place – excitement, curiosity, discovery and responsibility ... children preparing for SATs (national tests) at 11 are made to work out three stock stories and six characters in the year before the exam ... the consequence is that a test intended to measure and encourage creativity and storytelling does precisely the opposite. (Russell 2005: 28)

Moreover, the examination boards readily admit that those who know more than the syllabus find it harder to do well.

The consequences of the mindless treadmill of examination preparation have been trenchantly spelt out by many other critics. As early as 1977 Muller complained that 'we are turning out highly skilled people who are literally barbarians' (cited in Frey 1992). In similar vein, Tomlinson has argued that if the forces of market competition remain dominant along with the language of marks and grades, performance indicators and league tables that sustain them, then 'teachers and their collaborators will have to keep the spirit of human kindness and vision of nobility alive in the catacombs while rendering unto Caesar the things that are Caesar's' (Tomlinson 1992).

Activity 3.3

Consider how far you agree with these quite extreme criticisms concerning the educationally damaging effects of increased levels of testing. What arguments could be made in favour of the positive effects of such developments?

Furthermore, despite the growing international obsession with raising standards, it is arguable that the assessment procedures in use have not kept pace even with current educational priorities. One reason for this is undoubtedly the traditionally Cinderella status of assessment as a professional concern such that educators at all levels of the system and in the majority of countries, are still almost completely illiterate concerning the development and use of sound assessment strategies in educational contexts, especially those that can promote learning. So great has the preoccupation with *measuring* become in order to provide data on which league tables of performance indicators can be published, that scant regard has often been paid to either the quality of these data or whether there might be rather more effective ways of both raising standards and providing for accountability.

A report from the US National Council on Educational Standards and Testing (1992), for example, asserted that 'standards, and assessments linked to the standards, can become the cornerstone of the fundamental systemic reform necessary to improve schools', a belief in the power of examinations to lead to some kind of educational golden age that Winner (cited in Madaus and Kellaghan 1991: 23) describes as equivalent to the 'optimistic technophilia' of the last two centuries. There is no evidence to support either the belief in the power of examinations *by themselves* to raise standards or the associated belief in market forces as a way of raising standards through the provision of assessment information. Indeed, there is growing evidence that while such policies may be successful in 'getting the scores up', they are also widening the gap between rich and poor since low educational achievement and staying on at school rates remain a stubborn indicator of a range of other social inequalities (Wheeler et al. 2005).

Such evidence as is available suggests that it is the quality of teaching itself and the learning climate created in the classroom which are of critical importance in raising the standard of learning outcomes (Mortimore et al. 1998). Stiggins (2004) contrasts some of these mistaken, but very widely held beliefs about assessment with some more constructive and evidence-based beliefs:

> **Mistaken belief 1:** High-stakes standardized tests are good for all students because they motivate them to learn.
>
> **More productive belief 1:** High-stakes tests without supportive classroom assessment environments harm struggling students.
>
> **Mistaken belief 2:** It is the instructional decisions of adults that contribute the most to student learning and school effectiveness.
>
> **More productive belief 2:** Students are crucial instructional decision-makers whose information needs must be met.

Strategies which have as their core strengthening the accountability of individual teachers and schools through various forms of assessment of performance do not necessarily offer teachers any insight about what to do in terms of changing their practice to achieve the higher standards sought.

Summary

In this chapter, we have briefly reviewed the remarkably extensive and consistent evidence that the technologies we currently employ in educational assessment are at best limited and, all too often, downright flawed. We have explored why it is that the world clings so tenaciously to its belief in the results of educational assessment in terms of the enormous significance of its perceived legitimacy among both those who are judged and those who use these judgements. We have considered the price that is being paid for such trust, both in terms of individual injustices and in terms of missed opportunities for the pursuit of more relevant and fruitful forms of learning. If, historically, the practice of educational assessment has been largely driven by a perceived need to *measure* individual capacity, there is now a widely recognized need for assessment practices to be harnessed to *promote* such capacity – and indeed, to help create new kinds of capacities.

As was suggested above, problem-solving ability, personal effectiveness, thinking skills and willingness to accept change are typical of the general competences straddling cognitive and affective domains that are now being sought in young people. Integral to many of these attributes, is the capacity for individuals to be self-aware and to be capable of identifying what they need to learn. As we shall see in the next chapter, there have been very significant developments in the wider world that have profound implications for the goals and practice of education. These include:

- The knowledge explosion and the growing mass of information to which it has given rise, together with the advances in technology to store and communicate it.
- The change in the nature of employment away from manufacturing towards information-based and service industries requiring higher-order thinking and problem-solving skills.
- The growth of a global economy and global interdependence and the increase in the numbers of those who live and work in multicultural and multilingual environments.
- The move towards greater equity and towards greater participation in decision-making.
- The demand for greater accountability and transparency. (Clark 1994: 36)

It is becoming increasingly apparent, however, that until we develop new kinds of assessment procedures that can relate to this wide range of skills and attitudes, not only will it be impossible to produce valid judgements about the success of the *educational enterprise as a whole* in terms of its goals, but also it will help to guarantee that certain desired educational outcomes will be neglected in the classroom. The possible consequences of such neglect and the urgency of change are issues that we address in the next chapter.

Meanwhile, it is appropriate to conclude this discussion of 'the myth of measurement' with the words of an early critic of the new assessment technology who saw even at the turn of the twentieth century what the price would be for schools, teachers and students if the developing provision of mass educational provision became dominated by the language of marks and grades and the narrow horizons imposed by formal examinations. Sadly, his words fell on stony ground. But they remain as true today as they were nearly a hundred years ago.

A school that is ridden by examination incubus is charged with deceit. All who become acclimatized to the influence of the system, pupils, teachers, examiners, employers of labour, parents, MPs and the rest, fall victims and are content to see themselves with outward and visible signs, class lists, orders of merit, as being of quasi-divine authority. (Edmund Holmes 1911)

Key references

Lee-Smith, M. (1990) *The Role of Testing in Elementary School*. SCE Technical
Report 321. Los Angeles, CA: Arizona State University, pp. 521–42.

Satterly, D. (1994) Chapter 2 in Harlen, W. (ed.) *Enhancing Quality in Assessment*. London: Paul Chapman.

Stiggins, R. (2004) 'New Assessment Beliefs for a New School Mission'. *Phi Delta Kappan* (September), pp. 22–7.

Useful websites

www.fairtest.org/

The National Centre for Fair and Open Testing (FairTest) works to end the misuses and flaws of standardized testing and to ensure that evaluation of students, teachers and schools is fair, open, valid and educationally beneficial.

4

A World in Thrall: International Assessment Regimes

Earlier in this book, I argued that one reason for the immense importance of educational assessment is that it is a truly international phenomenon. Today, there is no country in the world that does not have a system of formal examinations and certification. Contemporary forms of educational assessment are a central feature of the colonial legacy – along with western-style schools. Many countries have looked to the former colonial powers either to provide their public examinations or to support the development of their own national examination bodies modelled on similar lines.

Today, an increasingly mobile and global society is putting a premium on qualifications that have international currency. This trend is thus further reinforcing the global reach of current forms of educational assessment. If western-style examinations and tests were one of the earliest features of globalization, they have now become one its most pervasive and powerful engines.

It is therefore important to consider the impact of current assessment regimes on an international basis. How well are they meeting the needs of different types of society and what is their impact?

The Current Situation

In 1994 Mackintosh conducted a comparative study for the International Association of Educational Assessment and the International Bureau of Education of current theories and practices in assessing students' achievements at primary and secondary level in ten countries – Australia, Bahrain, England and Wales, Guatemala, Israel, Malaysia, Namibia, Poland, Scotland and Slovenia. It is hard to imagine a more diverse range of countries in terms of culture, political structure, stage of development and educational tradition. Yet the survey found a remarkably similar picture in all these countries. A picture, moreover, that was not encouraging:

> it is a picture that shows that assessment results are much more widely used for selection than they are for diagnosis – a situation that is widely accepted; that most of the assessment in current use is restricted in scope and operates within a relatively restricted curriculum framework; that the provision of assessment is not adequately equipping young people going into the world after school and is not adequately addressing the problems of cultural diversity, gender bias, special needs or gifted students. Finally it shows that there is remarkably little pressure for change. (Mackintosh 1994: 32)

Unfortunately, the findings of this study have been borne out by many other international reviews.

Mackintosh suggests that the main reason for the apparent desire to retain the status quo in assessment in all these countries, appears to be the purposes to which the results of assessment are put. The most common use of assessment found in this study was for selection purposes, followed by national monitoring with diagnosis of an individual's learning needs a poor third. In short, in a situation of increasingly high-stakes assessment for both individuals and institutions, both policy-makers and teachers are likely to lack the will to change. High-stakes assessment, as we have seen, tends to emphasize reliability or dependability as the overriding need in all formal assessment. The desire for simple (i.e. cheap and readily manageable) reliable assessment is further reinforced by concerns about equity and security, both of which are crucial to the publicly perceived legitimacy and, hence, acceptability of high-stakes assessment for selection.

Thus, suggests Mackintosh, the result of the recent massive and global growth of high-stakes assessment is substantially to lower the risk-taking properties of all parties involved in the assessment process, and to stress instead the need for simplicity, practicability and technical reliability. In many countries in the developing world these generic pressures are further reinforced by the additional problems of cheating and of the need to provide assessment cheaply for large numbers of students. These pressures serve further to strengthen the tendency to fall back on machine-markable, multiple-choice approaches to testing. China's new national examination system provides a very good example in this respect since the sheer scale of the enterprise and the very high stakes involved for individuals makes it difficult to conceive of an alternative approach in the current international context (Lewin 1997).

Yet another pressure is the fact that more and more people are taking formal examinations and tests. This results in growing pressure to maintain the reliability of tests as a way of defending their publicly perceived standard. Sadly, as Mackintosh's study clearly shows, the result is an approach to assessment that is less and less appropriate for most of those taking it: 'One of the great ironies of assessment is that where the need is greatest for progressive, innovative curricula, so the pressure is also greatest for recognisable and comparable forms of assessment' (Mackintosh 1994).

Assessment Dilemmas

Here we have the nub of the problem to which there is no easy solution. Assessment and examination practices are subject to a series of fundamental dilemmas, which all countries must resolve in terms of a balance between rival goods. Eckstein and Noah (1993), in an international comparative study of examinations, summarized these dilemmas as follows:

- democratization versus devaluation
- uniformity versus diversity
- technology versus validity
- efficiency versus professional autonomy.

The first dilemma concerns the problem of widening access. It is difficult to adapt examinations which were originally designed to accredit a small secondary-school elite, and perhaps to select the even smaller subsection of these individuals aspiring to enter higher education, for use on a much wider scale, without some devaluation of the credentials gained. A good example of this is the current inability of the English A-level examinations to discriminate sufficiently between candidates for the purposes of university entrance, where large numbers of candidates now get 'perfect' (3 A Grades) scores (Tomlinson 2004). This is because an examination designed in the early 1950s for some 30 per cent of the age cohort is now being taken by more than twice that percentage. France is facing a similar phenomenon in which the tradition of formal equality among institutions and diplomas at a given level is being eroded by the emergence of new academic hierarchies which are a reflection of the 'qualification inflation' that is in turn a reflection of the competitive pressure within mass education societies. The result, as Wolf (2002: 15) suggests, is 'In a high unemployment economy, French young people have created a hierarchical, competitive tertiary system with strong similarities to our own'.

The second dilemma concerns the necessity of providing for comparability between examinations while, at the same time, providing certification procedures that reflect the increasing diversity of the secondary school population and curriculum content.

The third dilemma concerns the issue of the understandable desire to make use of new technologies of testing without adversely constraining the content of schooling, given the very significant 'washback' effect of assessment on what is taught and how.

Last, but not least, is the impact of the progressively increasing desire on the part of governments to provide not only value for money and efficiency in the public assessment system, but also to make it cheaper, as it becomes an increasingly large-scale enterprise. Despite the very real and acknowledged benefits, both for teaching and learning and for teachers themselves, of ceding a substantial degree of responsibility for assessment to teachers, most governments have either steadfastly resisted it or found it very difficult to introduce. This is partly because of the perceived expense of training and supporting teachers and of providing for moderation and partly because of the pressure of public opinion and fears about cheating.

Like Mackintosh, Noah and Epstein found the contemporary assessment dilemmas that they identified to be remarkably constant across the eight countries which they compared – China, England and Wales, Germany, France, Japan, Sweden, the USA and the former USSR.

Activity 4.1

Consider the dilemmas identified above. Is it possible to identify an education system in which these dilemmas have been resolved or to imagine one in which they might be?

Qualification Inflation

A more recent international review of secondary-school examinations by Wolf and Bakker (2001) suggests these problems are not, in any way, diminishing. As mass educational provision is increasingly becoming a characteristic of higher education, as well as of the primary and secondary stages of schooling, so this has put new pressures on the examinations and tests at the end of secondary education. Although the countries in Wolf and Bakker's study had significant differences in their examination practices at this level, all of them – France, Israel, Italy, the Netherlands, Slovenia and the United States – have struggled to find a fair and practicable system of examinations for selection to higher education, and none so far has found it. So, while recognizing the inevitable inaccuracies in all assessment procedures, most countries have nevertheless settled for the traditional examination as the most publicly defensible and, hence, legitimate and acceptable method of regulating entry to higher education.

All the countries studied by Wolf and Bakker also suffered from pressures generated by the expansion of higher education itself in terms of the impact of the growth in student numbers on the curriculum and on students' and teachers' learning priorities at this level. Increasingly it seems, even in higher education, the business of teaching and learning is becoming instrumental, with the goal of gaining a particular qualification tending to squeeze out more esoteric educational priorities.

An awareness of the problems created by the domination of assessment procedures was recognized in Dore's classic 1976 study, *The Diploma Disease*, in which Dore described an increasing credentialist spiral that was gripping nations across the world. In this study of a number of different developing and developed countries, he observed: 'the systematic sacrifice of creativity, curiosity and the development of the whole person to a ritualistic, tedious, anti-educational reduction of education to mere qualification learning' (p. 185).

Figure 4.1 is Dore's original summary of the forces that combine to produce 'the diploma disease'.

Thus, here we can identify once again the arguments of Chapter 3 concerning the profound impact of assessment procedures on educational priorities and the tendency for them to lead to 'teaching the test', perhaps even more in those countries where opportunities are more limited and educational success is perceived to be the key to subsequent life-chances.

Twenty years later, reflecting on his 'diploma disease' theory, Dore is more measured in his judgement (Dore 1997). First he points to the unanticipated, and indeed unanticipatable, impact of political upheavals and more general international developments, such as monetarism. He points to significant differences between countries in the way that they have tackled the 'diploma disease', in some cases with a measure of at least temporary

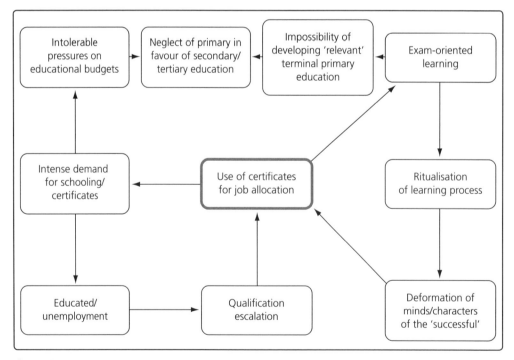

Figure 4:1

success. He also recognizes the validity of the argument that examinations do force children to learn many useful things that they otherwise might not have. In the end he questions how far any change in the nature of curriculum priorities or in the content of examinations, will ultimately affect the productivity of workers.

This indeed would appear to be one of the great ironies in the international obsession with educational standards and qualifications since so far it has proved impossible to establish any clear link between educational standards and economic performance (Robinson 1999; Wolf 2002). As long as governments *believe* that such a link exists, however, their priorities are unlikely to change.

Another international survey, this time by Little (2000), extends and deepens Dore's analysis through a review of educational assessment developments over the last 20 years in England, Japan, Sri Lanka, Kenya, Egypt and Australia and, in particular, in Cuba, Tanzania and China; three of the countries which at one time or another have embarked on radical reforms of the education–qualification–jobs nexus. As might be anticipated, she documents both commonalities and significant differences in the trajectories of these various countries in relation to assessment. Both the historical situation, culturally and institutionally of particular countries, and the specific events that have impacted on them, have led to differences of emphasis and practice in assessment. These are broadly in line with Eckstein and Noah's dilemmas.

Nevertheless, it is worth reiterating that the examination of 'the diploma disease' phenomenon 20 years on suggests that the importance of educational qualifications in the life-plans and chances of individuals, is rising in all the countries studied, except in Tanzania, where the level of improved access to employment possibilities as a result of certification appears not to be sufficient to prompt parents to invest in education. Little therefore concludes that: 'the influence of the pursuit of certificates on the quality of learning and teaching is more difficult to establish globally, than the influence of employment structures on the pursuit of the certificate' (1997: 9).

That the pursuit of certificates *conditions* the environment in which learning and teaching takes place is supported by all the country case studies. That it is the *major* determinant of the quality of teaching and learning is contested, however, in that the quality of teaching is not necessarily either helped or inhibited by the presence of particular assessment arrangements.

Activity 4.2

How far do you agree with the notion of 'the diploma disease'? What scope is there for educationally hungry countries to resist it?

The Global Role of Assessment

Perhaps the most interesting argument put forward by Little, however, is the relationship between assessment and globalization referred to briefly above. She argues that assessment is not only influenced by globalization in the search, for example, for more portable and internationally valid qualifications, but that it is also an influence on the process of globalization itself. Indeed this is one of the most significant, if least discussed, features of educational assessment as we know it today.

At the beginning of this chapter, I suggested that educational assessment – as it developed in the nineteenth century – was one of the major products exported during the colonial era. It helped shape the nature of educational provision in colonies around the world and led to many former British colonies, for example, having examination boards which were modelled very closely on those instituted by English universities such as Oxford, Cambridge and London in the nineteenth century.

Thus, perhaps, more than any other element of the apparatus of western forms of schooling, public examinations have served to shape global conceptions of how education should be organized and delivered on a mass basis. The result, as we have seen in this chapter, is a world in which it appears to be well-nigh impossible for the national education systems of individual countries to diverge significantly from the international obsession with examinations and the pursuit of certification for selection. Although the situation is worse in some countries than others, none are immune, it seems, to the infection of 'the diploma disease'.

Summary

Part Two of this book is entitled 'Assessment in its Social Context' because it has sought to show how the educational assessment practices with which we are familiar today have developed out of changing historical conditions and in response to new social pressures. In Chapter 2 we explored how novel pressures for the fair and transparent regulation of both opportunity and competence gave rise to a whole new industry of formal school examinations. The influence of this new industry was later supplemented by the advent of psychometric testing and the concepts of mental ability that underpinned much of it.

In Chapter 3 we examined some of the lessons to be learned from the huge volume of research that exists concerning how well educational assessment lives up to the aspirations we have for it. We reviewed some of the reasons why it is inevitably a human, rather than a scientific, activity, and hence its inevitable inaccuracies.

The significance of these limitations in a world in which educational performance –individually, institutionally and nationally – is increasingly at a premium, is, as Chapter

4 has described, a world in which no country finds itself able to resist the pervasive influence of formal educational assessment. Thus, despite the extensive evidence that exists concerning the technical limitations of formal educational assessment and, even more importantly, its constraining effect on educational innovation, we nevertheless find ourselves today in a world in which many countries, far from deploring this stranglehold, are enthusiastically embracing the extension of the educational assessment apparatus to the evaluation of institutions and systems as well.

The implications of this situation in relation to the novel educational challenges of the twenty-first century are serious as we discuss in the next and final chapter of Part Two.

Key references

Dore, R. (1976) *The Diploma Disease.* London: Allen and Unwin.

Little, A. (ed.) (1997) 'The Diploma Disease Twenty Years on'. *Assessment in Education* Volume 4, Number 1 (January).

Wolf, A. (2002) *Does Education Matter? Myths about education and economic growth.* London: Penguin.

Useful websites

http://www1.oecd.org/

The OECD (Organization for Economic Cooperation and Development) has 30 member countries and close relationships with 70 others. It produces internationally agreed instruments, decisions, studies and recommendations concerning international developments and issues in education.

The Contemporary Challenge

Chapter Outline

Through life there is learning;
Through learning there is life. (Maori proverb)

Time for a Change

Many countries are now beginning to recognize the unhelpful effects that the obsession with traditional forms of examination and testing are having. In 1999, for example, the South China *Morning Post* published a headline 'Exam Culture Is Failing our Students'. Other Asian regions are also now recognizing the limitations and indeed damage caused by the kind of obsession with studying for tests and exams that characterizes student orientations to learning, particularly in Asia but in other parts of the world as well. The following extracts from newspaper reports capture the stresses and strains that virtually all young people are now exposed to very aptly:

> *I'm Sorry I Nodded Off*
> *every exam season brings fresh concerns. This summer for instance has seen a zooming rise in the number of teenagers popping antidepressants and other pills to see them through'.* Donald Hiscock, *The Guardian*, 15 June 2004

Exam Fears Driving Teenagers to Prozac
the number of teenagers relying on drugs such as Prozac to see them through GCSEs
and A levels has soared, with prescriptions reaching 140,000 in less than a decade. Mark
Townsend, *The Observer Sunday*, 6 June 2004

The family, friends and teachers of Tina Dziki, a bright 15-year-old south London stu-
dent, are grief-stricken after she died last week as a result of taking an overdose. She
left a suicide note that described a number of troubles including anxiety about two
GCSE exams she was due to take a year early. The Guardian, 2 June 2004

Apart from the human cost of exams, the financial cost is also huge. In England, in
particular, which has possibly the most examined students in the world, the sheer scale of
the expenditure on examinations is very striking. As *The Guardian* newspaper reported
recently:

> The annual cost of exams and tests has risen to more than £200 million since Labour came to
> power – a 50% rise … Secondary age children are out of lessons for at least 46 weeks during
> their seven years of secondary education because of the test system and spend something like
> 150 hours sitting exams. English school pupils suffer the worst and take up to 105 tests and
> exams during their years at school. (Berliner 2003: 2)

Between the ages of 14 to 19, the average student will spend two and a half terms – more
than 30 weeks – preparing for, taking and recovering from examinations. Meanwhile the
average tertiary college will be spending £500,000 per year on entry fees for external examinations, the average school, £150,000 to £200,000 – the second biggest call on the budget
after teachers' salaries (Tomlinson 2004).

However, the motivation to address the impact of current forms of educational
assessment is not typically rooted in worries about the suffering that excessive concern
with examination results imposes on students themselves, although in places like Japan
this so-called 'examination hell' has long been recognized as a major problem. Nor, surprisingly perhaps in this cash-strapped age, is it driven by a desire to save money, despite the
enormous amount of resources that is now devoted to educational assessment in its various
guises. Rather, such pressure as there is for change arises from the recognition that society
as a whole is now moving into a new era. This is the era of the 'knowledge society' and
'the learning age' in which young people will need to be prepared to cope with a rapidly
changing world.

It has long been the case that educational institutions have sought to inculcate a wider
range of dispositions than just academic knowledge and skills. As early as 1853 Cardinal
Newman advocated that the 'university man' should possess cognitive communication and
interpersonal skills and 'certain affective qualities' (cited in Baud and Salchikov 2004). Yet,

though we know fairly well how to help people master skills, how you help people make progress in these other areas is much more complicated. 'Moreover, what employers are looking for is less competence and more confidence' (Bennett et al. 2000). As was suggested earlier, it is widely agreed that the kinds of skills students will need are self-awareness as the basis for individual target-setting, the capacity to choose between different options in a complex and unpredictable environment, creativity in order to be able to generate new solutions to problems and self-reliance, in short, 'knowing what to do when you don't know what to do' (Claxton 2002). Thus, for example, Singapore has radically redesigned its curriculum to free up a substantial element of time in which the creativity of students can be developed.

It seems likely that there will need to be radical changes in both the curriculum and in teaching methods but, most of all, in assessment, if the desired changes in the orientation of students to their learning and in their skills are to be brought about. Since, as I have argued, it is widely believed that the economic prosperity of any given society is likely to depend on the existence of young people who can profit from the significant array of new educational opportunities now opening up, it is not surprising that governments around the world are now putting great emphasis on vocational preparation and the inculcation of work-related, generic skills.

Towards a Learning Society ...

In 1995 Murphy and Broadfoot summed up the current pressure for change as follows:

> Equally central to this vision (a whole society committed to learning) is the need to equip individuals with the skills and resources they need to become self-reliant and self-motivated learners; the skill to assess what has and has not been learned; to evaluate personal learning needs and goals; to choose the appropriate route in order to achieve these goals is vital to the vision of a learning society. It is for this reason that recent decades have seen an explosion of interest in developing new student-centred forms of recording learning achievements – learning logs, portfolios, profiles, records of achievement and personal action plans – a host of different international initiatives which are geared towards this end. (p. 249)

This message is also strongly argued by Guy Claxton: 'The only valid preparation for an unknown future must comprise ... the development of an assured, astute approach to learning itself.' He argues the need for a 'learning curriculum' that accompanies the familiar 'subject curriculum like a shadow'. 'As students are engaged in mastering particular bodies of knowledge, skill and understanding, so they are developing, often at a less conscious, less intentional level, a set of dispositions, qualities and capabilities, that together determine their capacity for effective lifelong learning.' In short, he suggests, 'to be an effective lifelong learner one must be ready, willing and able to learn' (Claxton 1999).

The validity of Claxton's argument has been publicly recognized in many policy documents from governments around the world. In 1996, for example, the UK Department for Education and Employment/Cabinet Office wrote in its 'Competitiveness: Creating the Enterprise Centre of Europe' White Paper, 'The UK's overall competitiveness ultimately depends on the knowledge, motivation, ability and enterprise of its people'. In the same year the major review of qualifications for 16–19 year-olds in England, conducted by Sir Ron Dearing argued that:

> The only strategy for a nation seeking to maintain and enhance a high standard of living lies in concentration on advanced products and services, a high level of motivation, challenging and constantly improving standards of achievement, and competitiveness based on a highly educated, well trained and adaptable workforce.

But how is this highly trained and adaptable, motivated and enterprising workforce to be achieved? How far does the present system of assessment match these goals? Let us first remind ourselves of the kinds of skills and attributes that employers say they want. The following list, which was produced by the Institute of Personnel Managers as early as 1984, is very similar to that cited in Chapter 1 which was produced in 2004.

In most jobs employers look for:

- literacy
- numeracy
- communication
- organization of own work
- working with colleagues
- working with people in authority
- analytical ability and problem-solving
- judgement and decision-making
- adaptability
- responsibility, self-awareness, maturity.

New World, New Skills?

At a time when employers are saying that they need individuals who can think, solve problems and work in teams (Tomlinson 2004) we are increasingly subjecting the workers of tomorrow to tests and exams that require cramming, the reproduction of existing knowledge and individual competition (Broadfoot et al. 2000). As *The Times Higher*

Education Supplement put it: 'These are things that can't be covered by the straight-forward word 'skills'. The things that employers value are qualities and dispositions' (2004: 11).

Activity 5.1

Do you think it is possible to assess these 'other' qualities in a reliable and valid way? If so in what ways might this be done?

As will already be apparent, one of the main causes of this problem is a failure to recognize the incompatibility of 'the standards agenda' with its emphasis on the use of traditional tests for high-stakes purposes, with the pursuit of twenty-first-century skills and learning orientations. This apparent lack of awareness of the significance of these policy contradictions has in turn tended to inhibit efforts to create alternative assessment technologies. The problem is further compounded by the sheer complexity of finding suitable ways of assessing complex and ephemeral educational objectives such as creativity, practical knowledge, social skills and the like.

Indeed, despite the acknowledged importance of these abilities, relatively little is known about them: how they develop, what factors influence that development and how they are related to more traditional measures. It is now readily accepted that intelligence is, at the very least, composed of a number of different strands. Perkins (1995), for example, identifies three distinct kinds of intelligence: the fixed, neurological intelligence linked to IQ tests; the specialized knowledge and experience that individuals acquire over time and reflective intelligence, the ability to become aware of one's own mental habits and transcend limited patterns of thinking.

Although all of these forms of intelligence function simultaneously, it is reflective intelligence, he argues, that affords the best opportunity to amplify human intellect. Another leading American psychologist, Howard Gardner, also argues that individuals have very different strengths and ways of engaging with the world. Put perhaps too simply, his work argues that each person has a range of intelligences spanning linguistic, logical or mathematical musical, spatial, kinaesthetic (bodily, physical), interpersonal and intrapersonal dimensions (Gardner 1999).

Arguably even more important, however, is the growing recognition of the key role that emotions play, both in learning and in effective work-performance. Since Goleman's best-selling work on *Emotional Intelligence* took the world by storm in the 1990s, it has become increasingly widely accepted that to be successful in life requires a very much wider range of skills, especially interpersonal skills, than those that commonly form the focus of formal educational assessment in relation to academic curricula.

Goleman (1999) himself suggests that:

> the emotional brain learns in a different way to the rational brain. While a classroom setting and textbooks may be appropriate for learning technical skills, they are almost useless for learning to behave in a more emotionally intelligent fashion … the emotional brain re-shapes itself through repeated experience, that's why I'm against testing for EQ as we do for IQ.

As we shall see in Part Four, where learners are engaged and interested in a particular activity either because it is intrinsically interesting to them or because it has a clear connection with a significant personal agenda, their capacity to learn is typically greatly increased. But these important questions about the 'what' and the 'how' of learning for today's world are topics that the dominance of traditional forms of assessment have made it very difficult to address.

The central message of much recent work by both popular and academic psychologists is that if we want young people to develop capacities which include emotional intelligence and other so-called twenty-first-century skills, we have to find ways both to teach these and, above all, to assess them. If such skills, dispositions and qualities are not assessed, they will not be valued by students and taught by teachers, however much exhortation emanates from governments.

Assessment: The Ultimate Turn-Off?

At the present time, we appear to lack the robust assessment technologies for the summative testing of such skills in traditional testing modes. Added to this is the evidence now emerging about the active inhibition that much conventional assessment provides to the achievement of a society based on more and better learning. For example, a review of the research literature relating to the impact of summative assessment on student motivation by Harlen and Deakin-Crick (2003) found that many students around the world are significantly discouraged and demotivated by the anxiety that summative testing produces. They also found that the experience of failure that must be, by definition, the fate of many also served to demotivate many students. Indeed, more general research into learning and the brain shows consistently that stress and anxiety inhibit learning (Csikszentmihalyi *et al.* 1993). The term 'down-shifting' describes the process when the brain experiences threat or fear and down-shifts to the primitive state of flight or fight, where learning is much less possible.

The policy dilemma is, hence, very clear. On the one hand, there is a strong international movement towards finding ways of building a knowledge-based society and of fostering both lifelong learning and new types of learning. At the same time, the rapid rise in recent years of the much greater use of very traditional forms of examinations and testing for the purposes of monitoring standards and providing for accountability, appears to be working directly against this 'knowledge society' agenda.

Activity 5.2

How far are current assessment systems helping or hindering the achievement of these new educational goals? In what ways ought they to change and how far do you think this is possible?

Warming up or Cooling out?

A high-participation and high-achievement society is now increasingly being seen around the world as the foundation of both individual and national prosperity. Thus it is now generally recognized that the young people who were progressively weeded out of the education system in the past, when relatively few highly educated workers were required, in today's world need to be motivated to want to participate to the highest possible levels, rather than being excluded from educational opportunity.

Thus, whereas one of the principal reasons for the creation of early examination systems was the need to devise a mechanism that would provide an acceptable basis for progressively *excluding* all but a tiny minority from reaching the pinnacle of the education system, now societies' priorities are typically rather different. In a very real sense we are moving from a world in which educational opportunity had to be *rationed,* a world in which, as a consequence, providing for fair competition between individuals in a way perceived to be legitimate was of overwhelming importance, to a world in which educational opportunities are plentiful – at least in developed countries. The challenge now is thus rather to equip and motivate individuals to take full advantage of these opportunities. At the same time, however, there is likely to be a continuing, and probably increasing, need for selection as more and more individuals find themselves equipped to compete for the choicest prizes.

Here, once again, we find ourselves on the horns of a dilemma. On the one hand, there is the continuing need for robust and apparently legitimate assessment mechanisms that can provide the fine discrimination needed to ration access to the most coveted opportunities – access to the most prestigious universities, for example, or to the most sought-after jobs or professional training. Given the increasing 'massification' of higher education, in particular, it is clear that the tools currently in use are already hardly capable of bearing the strain, in terms of their ability to discriminate sufficiently finely between what are often huge numbers of applicants (Gauthier 2004). In England, for example, it is now not uncommon for a popular course in a prestigious university to attract up to 40 applicants per place, many of whom are more than qualified for it. In order to discriminate more finely while sustaining trust in the mechanisms used, universities are seeking to develop new kinds of tests which will not only provide for finer discrimination than examination grades, but also be more valid in terms of the subject to be studied and thus have greater predictive power. Equally the government is mooting a new A* grade for the English Advanced Level university entrance examination for the same purpose.

But, while these new assessment hurdles are being created, there is simultaneously a growing need to create a very different kind of assessment apparatus that is supportive and encouraging, flexible and transparent. Such assessment needs to facilitate the development of the global employment market by providing readily understood and calibrated testimony to an individual's skills and achievements. Complementing this developing agenda is the need for individuals to be motivated and encouraged by their experience of assessment so that they want to go on learning. Last but not least, there is a need for a new kind of assessment that can support students in developing their skills as learners and their ability to manage themselves and their careers to best effect. In short, contemporary assessment priorities are:

- **Selection** – providing a mechanism that is perceived as fair for fine discrimination between candidates where there is intense competition.
- **Certification** – providing portable, transparent and internationally calibrated system of credit.
- **Motivation** – providing formative and summative feedback that is constructive and confidence-building.
- **Personal development planning** – providing learners with the tools needed to train and support them in managing their lifelong learning.

Clearly, achieving a resolution of these different assessment priorities will be difficult. It will certainly require the creation and use of novel assessment technologies that are significantly different in form and purpose from those that were described in Chapter 2, for the origin of these was associated with the very different social and economic demands facing educational provision in the nineteenth century.

Unfortunately, so great is the current obsession with testing, that it has tended to narrow the vision of what is possible and desirable in assessment terms. It has also narrowed the vision of education itself to the point where education has become almost synonymous with vocational preparation and economic competitiveness. There is a terrible irony in this. At the very time when countries are most concerned with maintaining educational competitiveness and developing work-related skills, they are increasingly obsessed with using assessment tools which are significantly outmoded in terms of the priorities they were designed to address, and hence are incapable of supporting this policy agenda effectively.

In the following extract, Broadfoot and Pollard express this dilemma in relation to the impact of the English national curriculum and assessment arrangements which were introduced following the 1988 Education Act. Summarizing their conclusions from a nine-year study they argue:

> the combined effect of recent policy changes in assessment has been to reinforce traditionalist conceptions of teaching and learning which are associated with a greater instrumentalism on

the part of pupils. From this it can be argued that rather than acquiring lifelong learning skills and attitudes, the effect of recent reforms has been to make pupils more dependent on the teacher and less ready to engage in 'deep' learning. (Broadfoot and Pollard 2000)

I have argued that the evolving nature of society and employment requires a change in educational priorities that are in line with new developments. Since assessment practices exert an overwhelmingly powerful influence on educational priorities and practices, for such changes to happen, assessment will need to change as well. In particular, there needs to be a change of emphasis from the use of assessment first and foremost for selection and prediction purposes towards its use, primarily, to support learning, and for recognizing achievement.

Summary: New Assessments for a New Era ...

In this chapter we have briefly reviewed the growing awareness on the part of societies around the world that the traditional focus of educational assessment on testing knowledge and skills, often in a highly competitive way, is unlikely to deliver workers with the employment skills that the conditions of the twenty-first century are increasingly likely to require. Moreover, the personal and financial cost of established assessment approaches still appears to cut little ice in countries where such traditional forms of assessment appear to be the most robust and defensible mechanism for managing aspirations. Such green shoots of change that do exist are likely to reflect the realization that education systems are not delivering the necessary competencies.

Certainly, it would seem to be the case, as Coffield (1999) in his extensive research into lifelong learning has written, that: 'the most far reaching changes in pedagogy and forms of assessment will need to be introduced to respond to the needs of those most in need of lifelong learning ... but the main barriers are structural rather than individual' (p. 10). Therefore 'individual, institutional, and structural change should be introduced simultaneously' (p. 17).

However, at present, even if the desire for change becomes powerful, there are two significant barriers. The first is the lack of novel techniques to assess the less traditional skills and qualities such as leadership and creativity. The second is the parallel development of assessment as a policy tool to monitor and evaluate *systems and institutions*, in addition to its traditional role of evaluating individual achievement. In recent years, educational assessment has demonstrated its capacity to be a very effective instrument of government control and, hence, a powerful policy tool.

Thus, whether the structural changes needed to facilitate lifelong learning to which Coffield refers, will take place, must remain in doubt as long as governments show little sign of abandoning their current enthusiasm for using educational assessment to foster competition and to strengthen central control. For, as we shall see in the next section, it is difficult to reconcile the use of educational assessment in this way with the aspirations that have been identified in this chapter. Thus, the impact of what I have called in this book 'the quality agenda' represents yet another assessment dilemma which we shall explore in the next part of this book.

Key references

Broadfoot, P. (1998) 'Quality, Standards and Control in Higher Education: What price life-long learning?' *International Studies in Sociology of Education* Volume 8, Number 2, pp. 155–80.

Coffield, F. (ed.) (1999) *Thinking Truth to Power*. Bristol: The Policy Press.

Gardner, H. (1999) *Intelligence Reframed: Multiple intelligences for the 21st century*. New York: Basic Books.

Useful websites

www.ceoforum.org/downloads/report

This is an example from the United States where an attempt is being made to align student assessment with educational objectives and include twenty-first-century skills. By 2003, every US state should match assessment to the new standards that include such skills.

www.unesco.org/education/educprog/tve/nseoul/docse/rstratve.html

The United Nations Educational Scientific and Cultural Organization (UNESCO) recognizes the educational challenges of the twenty-first century. Career, educational and labour market information and assessment.

Part Three
ASSESSMENT AS A POLICY TOOL

The Evaluative Gaze 6

Enter Evaluation

In Chapter 1 we considered the nature and purpose of educational assessment. In a book which is concerned with assessment at every level of educational activity – classrooms, institutions, systems and international comparisons – it is appropriate to include a brief discussion of other types of evaluative activity that are also manifestations of assessment. The term 'evaluation', in particular, is frequently used almost interchangeably with the term 'assessment' though it has some quite specialized applications. The word 'evaluation' makes explicit the central aspect of any assessment activity, namely, that it is concerned with values and the act of valuing.

Evaluation as a term is often used to refer to a particular genre of research activity concerned with the systematic judgement of the success of particular programmes and initiatives. Evaluation as a particular subfield of research first came to prominence in the area of curriculum development. From the mid-1970s onwards there was a major growth in the use of formal evaluation studies in relation to new policies and programmes. This period also saw the beginnings of a more generic use of evaluation as part of the burgeoning accountability movement discussed later, which was expressed, for example, in the notion of institutional self-evaluation.

With the advent of what I refer to in the next chapter as 'the quality agenda' – namely, the growing importance of assessment for monitoring the quality of educational provision

– evaluation has now become an integral part of the fabric of public life. It is an almost unquestioned requirement of publicly funded programmes and in most contemporary administrative and managerial practices.

There are many motivations for evaluation. Perhaps the simplest is the pragmatic desire to identify the effects of a particular set of practices. Overlaid on this is often the desire to establish cost-efficiency and effectiveness and, increasingly, the desire to establish whether an intervention is making things better. Equally there are many potential foci of evaluative activity. Given its contemporary importance as a form of assessment, it is appropriate to try to define 'evaluation' a little more precisely.

A Definition of Evaluation

As suggested above, at its simplest we may define evaluation as 'the process of obtaining information about the values and effects of educational activities' (Macdonald 1979: 5). This very broad definition of evaluation may be contrasted with, for example, a definition of accountability, which is a much more specific concept, namely, 'the condition in which individual role holders are liable to review and the application of sanctions if their actions fail to satisfy those with whom they are in accountability relationships' (Kogan 1986: 25).

However, the words 'evaluation', 'review', 'appraisal', 'audit' and so on, tend to be used very loosely and interchangeably with 'assessment' depending on the particular focus. Nevertheless, there are significant nuances of difference in what the terms mean. As has been suggested, *evaluation* is a very general term that is used to describe any activity by an institution or educational authority where the quality of provision is to be the subject of systematic study. *Review*, on the other hand, is a more retrospective activity implying the collection and examination of evidence and information. *Appraisal,* which is most typically used in relation to individual professionals, usually involves the forming of qualitative judgements about a person and typically embodies the notion of dialogue. *Assessment* is probably the most hard-nosed of all these approaches since it tends to involve more numerical data and be based on explicit criteria.

Fundamental to all these activities, however, is the making of judgements since this is what any evaluative activity is about. Having said this, in terms of the key assessment questions identified in Chapter 1, the emphases are likely to be quite different. The purposes for which the judgements are being used (the 'why' question); the focus of the evaluation (the 'who' and 'what' questions), the timing (the 'when' question) and the approach adopted (the 'how' question) will, of course, be variable. Particularly important in this respect is likely to be the outcome of the activity (the 'with what effect?' question).

The evidence collected may be 'soft' in that it is descriptive and qualitative, or 'hard' in that it is in numerical form and more quantitative. It may be 'ipsative' in relation to the individual's or institution's previous performance, as is typical, for example, of institutional self-evaluation schemes, or 'criterion-referenced' in relation to a given standard. Examples in this latter respect might include judgements in relation to a particular accreditation such as the right to award particular qualifications or the award of particular 'kite-marks' of quality. In another context, systems of hotel quality rating provide a good example in this respect.

Or again, the focus may be norm-referenced, involving some comparison in terms of relative performance to other persons or institutions. The aim may be to identify, for example, 'the best' and 'the worst' as is so often the focus when such data are used for 'league tables'. In some cases, the exercise in evaluation may involve some combination of all of these purposes. Where this is so, it can frequently lead to tensions and on occasions, to some of the worst abuses of assessment activity since, as should by now be apparent, it is very difficult to design any kind of evaluative procedure or system that is capable of fulfilling the criteria of 'fitness for purpose' for several different functions at once.

A Question of Purpose

A pervasive and often unfortunate feature of assessment and evaluation activities is the use of judgements generated for one purpose to be used for another. Thus, for example, data concerning the performance of individual students through public examinations may be used to evaluate institutional quality. These judgements are then in turn used to generate league tables of school performance. However, in transitions between criterion- and norm-referenced approaches and formative and summative purposes, there is considerable scope for the issue of 'fitness for purpose' to be obscured. The result, as I argue in this chapter, is a number of, at best unhelpful, and at worst, downright damaging assessment practices.

Moreover, as the importance of such evaluative activity for individuals, institutions and indeed whole education systems has steadily increased in recent years, becoming more 'high-stakes' in terms of both educational competitiveness and growing pressures for accountability, so its impact has become correspondingly greater. Evaluation studies, which once would have been conducted on a 'need to know' basis, are now increasingly likely to be associated with targets and penalties, whether this is for individuals or institutions.

Thus, for example, in England, students' results in the GCSE and A-level examinations are aggregated on a school basis and used both as an element in school inspection on a criterion-referenced basis, but also in government-published and widely publicized 'league tables'. Ostensibly designed to facilitate parental choice, the result is to 'name and shame' less successful institutions. Similar practices are used for a host of other institutions ranging from Local Education Authorities to hospitals. The serious problems with such practices are discussed in detail in the next chapter.

One result that is very clear is that the issue of 'fitness for purpose' – which I have argued in this book, is one of the most important definitions of quality in assessment practice – becomes correspondingly more important as the evaluation becomes more 'high-stakes'. Thus those who decide to institute such evaluative activities bear a heavy responsibility for thinking through their fitness for the intended purpose, including the range of potential consequences that may follow.

Some Key Questions

But, whatever the evaluation's ostensible purpose, it is important to recognize that any such evaluative activity is almost inevitably political. Even in the assessment of individual students, the political dimension is important. Though it may seem to be largely concerned with issues of public trust and acceptability, these aspects often translate into quite explicit features of party politics. In England, for example, the recommendations of successive reports on the reform of the A-level examination during recent decades – such as the 1988 Higginson Report and the 2004 Tomlinson Report were both almost immediately rejected by the prevailing political regime because of the perceived popularity with voters of the A-level examination. The 2004 Tomlinson Report, which argued for the urgently needed broadening of the certification system to integrate academic and vocational achievements and to recognize a wider range of skills which we have explored in this book, was largely rejected within a few days as an election loomed, although some issues raised by the report have been revived since.

Where the evaluation in question concerns more general programmes and initiatives, the process can never be free of contextual factors and the influence of the different perspectives of various stakeholders. Although such differences will occasionally be expressed as very overt power struggles, they may well be equally, or indeed even more significant, when the interests involved are not overtly articulated. The following list of questions relating to the design and outcomes of an evaluation make this point clear.

- Of what is the evaluation being undertaken?
- Who is sponsoring the evaluation?
- Who is carrying out the evaluation?
- Who is the evaluation for (audience)?
- How is the evaluation going to be carried out?
- What is the relationship between the evaluators and other stakeholders?
- Whose criteria of evaluation are to be applied?
- Who is the decision-maker? (Whose judgement counts?)
- What are the implications for those being evaluated?
- What rights do those being evaluated have?

- How is the evaluation to be being reported?
- Who will take action as a result of the evaluation?

Activity 6.1

This 'catechism' of key questions that should be answered in relation to any evaluation is based on a list by Harland (1986). Which questions do you think are the most important and why?

It is clear from some of these questions, such as 'who is the evaluation for?', that evaluation can never be a neutral process. Other questions concerning a particular evaluation that might be posed make this even clearer, for example:

- Who owns the data?
- Who produces the reports?
- What and who do they cover?
- Who gets the information?
- Is the information contextualized in taking into account inputs and processes as well as outcomes?
- Does it measure value added? (Harlen and Elliott 1982)

Activity 6.2

Think of an example of an evaluation with which you are familiar and consider these questions in relation to its conduct and outcomes. How far do you find yourself in agreement with the arguments being made here?

Unfortunately, such questions are rarely made explicit. Evaluations, like other aspects of assessment activity, are frequently not understood as the inevitably interpretive exercises they are. Moreover, teachers and other educators can find themselves caught up in demands for evaluation, which leave them little time to question its goals, methodologies or implications.

These points will become all too apparent in the following chapters of Part Three, in which we shall consider in more detail some of the manifestations of the recent growth in the quantity and range of evaluative activity within education systems. Part Three will explore the origins and significance of such practices, their faults and their positive potential, as well as analysing some of the defining features of 'the quality agenda'.

Summary

In this chapter I have addressed 'evaluation' as another manifestation of the act of collecting and interpreting data against a standard that also includes more familiar student-assessment practices. I have argued that evaluation, like assessment, is inevitably coloured by the values and perceptions that characterize all human interactions; hence it cannot be objective.

However, I have also argued that it can, and should, be as rigorous and as transparent as possible, conducted in the full knowledge of these potentially dangerous limitations. Like assessment, evaluation is a technique of considerable power to define and control. It therefore needs to be used with due *consideration* of its potential consequences and pitfalls. The 'quality agenda', which is the subject of the next chapter, represents a manifestation of the use of evaluation as a key policy tool. It provides an illustration of these arguments in the context of a series of developments that in recent decades have had the most far-reaching consequences for educational practice.

Key references

Harlen, W. (ed.) (1994) *Enhancing Quality in Assessment*. London: Paul Chapman.

House, E. (ed.) (1986) *New Directions in Educational Evaluation*. London: Falmer Press.

Murphy, R. and Torrance, H. (eds) (1987) *Evaluating Education: Issues and methods*. London: Harper and Row.

The Quality Agenda

A Shift Of Focus . . .

In earlier sections of this book, it was argued that many of the issues surrounding assessment of individual students' learning and achievement are also equally applicable to institutions. This is a fundamental point and one that has become increasingly apparent in recent years, as assessment has become more and more prominent as a policy tool. In Part Two I argued that student assessment developed powerfully in the nineteenth century in order to provide for control over individual aspirations, as well as to provide some measure of national coherence in terms of the content of education. The more recent advent of the use of assessment for system regulation and control reflects a similar, if later, realization that assessment procedures can also play a key role in the *management of educational provision as a whole,* as well as for the individuals within it.

In this chapter, I refer to these developments in broad terms as 'the quality agenda'. Pursuing the analysis of the preceding discussion of evaluation, this chapter explores the current policy fashion for using assessment to monitor and 'drive-up' standards on a national basis. In this chapter and the next, we shall consider some of the factors that have led to this development and some of its key characteristics and consequences. We also consider briefly some signs that a new stage of this agenda may be imminent. First, however, it is necessary to articulate a little more explicitly what we might mean by 'quality' in this context, since this is a term that, like 'standard', can have many different meanings. Indeed it is almost as difficult to define as it is widely used.

Defining 'Quality'

A working definition of quality is 'fitness for purpose'. Such a definition 'suggests that quality only has meaning in relation to the purpose of the product or service. Quality is thus judged in terms of the extent to which the product or service fits its purpose' (Harvey and Green 1993: 10). This notion of quality is quite remote from the idea of quality as something special, distinctive, elitist, conferring status, or difficult to attain. It is a functional definition of quality rather than an exceptional one.

If we pursue the first definition of quality, it becomes clear that the term is a relative one, defined by whatever purpose is being employed. In educational terms we cannot assume that there is consensus about purposes or priorities, except in the very broadest sense. Instead, we need to ask what type of quality is implicitly or explicitly being sought, as well as critiquing the various definitions of levels of quality that are in play in any particular assessment situation.

Elsewhere I have argued that it is the power *to define what counts as quality in education* that is the single most influential source of educational control, since it shapes the very way we think about issues (Broadfoot 1998a). One might argue that within the international discourse of education at the present time, assumptions around consumerism, education for economic competitiveness and the need for explicit accountability are all so taken for granted that they are rarely challenged or even problematized. The language of standards and targets, performance indicators and strategies, evaluation and transparency, is as pervasive as it is familiar. Yet, an 'audit society' (Power 1997) is neither inevitable nor necessarily desirable as we explore in the next section.

Assumptions of 'The Quality Agenda'

It is important to understand the nature of the changes that have been taking place as part of the more general project to understand the roles that educational assessment plays in society. We need to evaluate the strengths and weaknesses of these developments in terms of their capacity to contribute to improvements in the overall quality of both teaching and learning.

I have suggested that 'the quality agenda' is a powerful movement which broadly involves applying traditional approaches to educational assessment but at the level of the educational system itself. As such, the assumptions that underpin this agenda are broadly similar to the prevailing beliefs that have informed the use of educational assessment with individual students. In both cases, I suggest, these assumptions and beliefs remain still largely unexposed to critical examination. Some of the most important to examine are:

- That assessment is a neutral instrument that, with progressive technical refinement, is capable of measuring an individual's level of achievement objectively.
- That a test is a true measure of performance and thus of student learning.
- That institutional and national standards of educational achievement can similarly be measured.
- That, as with the marks and grades believed to incentivize students, the use of league tables and other public grading devices will incentivize institutions and so help to drive up educational standards.

> ## Activity Box 7.1
>
> How far do you agree with the list of assumptions underpinning the current use of assessment policy on a system-wide basis? Can you think of any other assumptions that might be added to this list?

Do Students' Results Reflect School Quality?

One of the defining features of 'the quality agenda' is the use of individual students' results as a currency to determine institutional quality. So widely used is this data that the phenomenon deserves our more sustained attention. So, do the test results of individual students represent a valid reflection of school quality? As has already been intimated results, certainly in the form of raw scores, are as much a reflection of the raw material with which the school has to work as they are of the quality of the school itself. The only fair comparison of school results is one where the other factors that influence student performance – home background, for example – are taken properly into account. This is clearly almost impossible to do.

The recent advent of interest in so-called 'value-added' approaches that are designed to measure the *improvement* of a given cohort of students, is clearly much fairer as well as being more informative in this respect. However, even 'value-added' measures still constrain the focus of quality to the criteria laid down for measurement and cannot embrace some of the more intangible, but perhaps most important, aspects of a school's ethos. These might include giving students a love of learning and the skills to become lifelong learners, or producing students who are likely to become worthwhile and caring future members of society.

Can One Test Do It All?

Another assumption which has been pursued for some considerable time is that it is possible to invent a system for national monitoring which can also be used for formative and summative assessment purposes of a more traditional kind. As will be apparent from the discussion in Chapter 1, there is likely to be a tension between the different purposes of assessment in terms of the key questions of who, what, when, how and why. Any attempt to provide for the full range of assessment purposes through one set of assessment procedures is almost doomed to meet some needs very inadequately.

In this book our focus has been not so much on whether the available evidence proves or disproves these assumptions. Rather it has been to argue that such evidence is inevitably partial because educational assessment is a complex human activity. Therefore any application of it is likely to have both positive and negative consequences depending on the context and the individual. Thus the most important thing is to be clear about the purpose of any particular assessment; and to think through the likely range of consequences. It is to some of these that we now turn.

Consequences of 'The Quality Agenda'

One fairly obvious result of the use of assessment for quality control of the education system at national level is that governments undoubtedly benefit from being seen to be tough on standards. Indeed, much US research, in particular, has suggested that many of the benefits of these policy initiatives are not so much practical, in the sense of the effects achieved, but political. There appears to be great symbolic value in testing which appeals to voters. Thus there is considerable potential benefit for governments to be seen to be championing standards and, hence, rigorous inspection and test-oriented policies. Indeed research suggests that there is currently more political mileage to be gained from an emphasis on external central control, high-reliability assessment and the operation of market forces than on an explicit concern with the educational benefits or otherwise of such policies. It is therefore not particularly surprising that a great deal more policy attention has been given to designing such assessments than to examining their consequences (Elwein et al. 1998).

By contrast, the consequences of 'the quality agenda' for individuals, especially students and teachers, seem much more negative. Elsewhere, I have referred to the kind of assessment used for national system purposes as 'categoric' because its rationale is to discriminate between either individuals or institutions in terms of their performance (Broadfoot and Pollard 2000). 'Categoric' assessment approaches provide the defining principle of contemporary education policy in many countries.

They are associated with the idea of 'performativity', a term originally conceived by the French philosopher Lyotard, but now widely used to describe the preoccupation with outputs, that characterizes a great deal of public life at the present time. Not surprisingly, 'categoric' assessment typically leads to behaviours designed to increase perceived 'performance' rather than to enhancing quality more generally. The familiar practice of teachers 'teaching the test', or of students 'trading for grades' using question spotting, are examples of 'performativity' which is a consequence of 'categoric' assessment. The characteristics of 'performativity' as expressed in educational assessment practices are set out in Figure 7.1 below.

In Chapter 4, we explored some of the international consequences of this kind of assessment as it is embodied in high-stakes public examinations and 'the diploma disease'. The consequences of the 'categoric assessment' associated with 'the quality agenda' are broadly similar, but there is also a very important difference. Whereas the effects of the 'performativity' associated with individual students' pursuit of examination success is widely deplored for the stress and curriculum narrowing it produces, this is an effect that is *deliberately sought* within the context of 'the quality agenda'. So strong is the prevailing belief in the power of competition to drive up standards, that other consequences appear to be an acceptable price of such policies.

Yet the negative impact of 'performativity' on students and teachers has been well-documented by researchers and widely deplored by educationists and many others who

ASSESSMENT FOR	
PERFORMATIVITY	**EMPOWERMENT**
celebrates intellectual convergence	celebrates intellectual divergence
encourages extrinsic motivation	encourages intrinsic motivation
educationally/socially divisive	helps widen opportunity
trusts 'objective' indicators of quality	trusts professional judgement
appears to raise standards	enhances learning

Figure 7.1 Different Priorities in Assessment

regret the consequent narrowing of the curriculum and the encouragement of test-taking behaviours in pupils. David Almond, the children's writer and himself a former teacher, provides an eloquent example of this view. Lamenting the stifling of creativity in schools, he predicted that in 50 years' time:

> the concentration on assessment, accreditation, targets, scores, grades, tests and profiles will be seen as a kind of madness ... The pedants are triumphant and go about the task of disintegrating our world like medieval philosophers they debate the exact weight to be given to every fragment – 15 per cent on this subject, 12.5 per cent on that, 5.7 per cent on the other. There's an arrogance at work, the arrogance that we know exactly what happens when someone learns something, that we can plan for it, that we can describe it, that we can record it and that if we can't do these things, then the learning doesn't exist. The arrogance leads us to concentrate on a particular kind of work, noses-to-the-grindstone treadmill kind of work, work that is observable, recordable and well-nigh constant ...
>
> Get kids into school fast. Get them assessed while they're in nappies, get them going in literacy clubs, numeracy clubs, lunchtime learning clubs, holiday learning clubs. Holidays, let's cut them. School day, let's lengthen it. Homework, one hour? No mate, let's make it two. Let's see them, children and teachers work, work, work, and let's get plenty of people watching them and recording them while they're at it. What would the assessors and records have made of Archimedes splashing happily about in his bath before he yelled 'Eureka!' What would they have made of James Watson snoring in his bed as he dreamt of the molecular structure of DNA? (Almond 1999: 12)

How such pressures to perform are experienced by children is well-illustrated by the child's eye view of the English national tests for 11 year-olds depicted in Figure 7.2.

The impact of the current intense testing culture on students and their learning is a very significant aspect of contemporary assessment practices and we shall return to it in Part Four. Perhaps less well-recognized, is the opportunity cost of such policies for the education system as a whole. In England, for example, it is proving very difficult for schools in disadvantaged areas to put in place the innovative, responsive and inclusive curriculum that the government is promoting as a key to raising standards and promoting social inclusion, within the context of a 'high-stakes', league-table-oriented culture (Halpin et al. 2004).

It is clear that the assumptions behind 'the quality agenda' and its consequences are both complex and ambiguous. Its implications are also continually changing as the mechanisms being used evolve. It is now time to consider some of these mechanisms more substantively and to look at the various factors that have underpinned the development of 'the quality agenda' in its contemporary form.

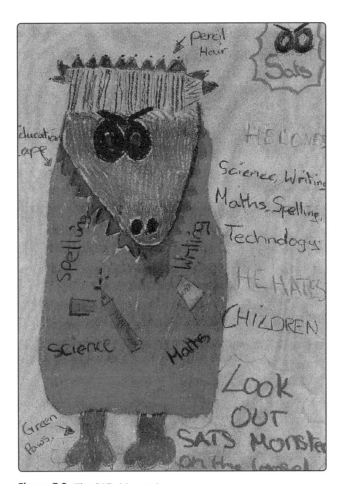

Figure 7.2 'The SATs Monster'

Explaining 'The Quality Agenda'

Many studies have been written which seek to document and explain the explosion of interest from the 1970s onwards in applying assessment to the evaluation of education provision. One early straw in the wind was the initiation of international comparative studies of students' achievement such as the International Educational Achievement Surveys (IEA Studies), which began at this time. These early studies, as well as more recent ones such as the 1990s' Third International Maths and Science Study (TIMSS) and the ongoing PISA Study (Brown 1999), have served to sensitize governments to the relative success of national education systems compared to those of other countries. In many countries they have awoken significant worries about prevailing national standards.

When such information is overlaid, as it was in the 1970s, with widespread and significant economic problems and recession on a global scale, it is likely to reinforce concerns that the education system is not delivering. A third straw in the wind was the growth during the 1970s and 1980s of the applied science of management and its central assumption that the generation of information will change things for the better by encouraging the cultivation of quality.

More recently, a growing enthusiasm for the cultivation of market forces in education, has woven these assumptions around management, into the very structure of many education systems. Thus, increasingly, policies are being developed that assume the ability of consumers to evaluate relative quality and hence to choose rationally between competing institutions.

While this may seem a very obvious point, in the early years of the twenty-first century, it is worth noting that in most education systems, until recently, much greater attention has been given to regulating and controlling the *input*s to education provision in terms of teacher supply, curriculum prescriptions, finance and general bureaucratic regulation, than to *outputs*. The shift of emphasis towards using the regulation of outputs as the key leverage point on educational delivery is as recent, as it is profound, in its effects (Neave 1989).

In an historical overview of European developments in this respect, Bonnet (2004) makes the standard distinction between input indicators such as percentage of national gross domestic product spent on education, process indicators such as class size and outcome indicators as indicated by test results. He suggests that outcome indicators have become of particular interest since they are felt to be the only one truly to reflect the real performance of education systems, yet at the same time, he argues they are probably the most unreliable because measuring performance is more subjective and influenced by cultural backgrounds, both national and personal.

Associated with the shift from a concern with inputs to a concern with outputs, has been a change of emphasis from raising the achievements of *individuals*, which has always been the concern of schools and teachers, to a concern with raising the overall levels of achievement in education *systems* though, of course, the one is a component of the other. By the same token individual learning needs have become subsumed within a broader concern in relation to the national economic interest.

The advent of a national curriculum in England and Wales, provides a classic illustration of this development. The 1988 policy initiative to introduce a national curriculum in a country that had never previously had one, was justified by the Conservative government of the time in terms of providing a common entitlement for all pupils. However, the effect was to change teachers' previous focus which, particularly in primary schools, had been on children's needs as individual learners in the context of the prevailing 'child-centred' educational ideology, towards a preoccupation with the delivery of standardized curriculum content in increasingly prescribed ways.

The subsequent development of the national literacy and numeracy strategies which were imposed on all state primary and secondary schools in England, provides a very clear illustration of this change of emphasis. Now, as well as curriculum *content* being laid down nationally, teaching *methods* – perhaps the most jealously guarded domain of professional practice – are also increasingly subject to central direction. Even more recently, the launch of citizenship as a new national curriculum subject in England, provides still further testimony to the government's now explicit desire to manage the operation of the English education system in some detail so that it will address what are perceived to be national educational priorities.

Given this shift from an essentially individualist approach to educational provision towards one where education provision has become a key plank of national policy, it is not surprising that the focus of evaluative activity has shifted from the earlier concern with the success of single initiatives and programmes in the 1970s and 1980s in favour of the evaluation of whole institutions and indeed whole systems. I refer to this shift as 'the quality agenda' since this title both evokes the management philosophy which underpins it, and also provides a shorthand for the assumptions informing it.

In the next section, we shall look briefly at some of the typical policy manifestations of 'the quality agenda'.

The Growth of National Monitoring

One of the first manifestations of the growing concern with the quality of education systems as a whole – and still among the most important – was the growing international fashion for national monitoring. Looked at it in historical context, before the 1980s in most countries there was no widespread availability of performance data. Typically, there were only statistics about inputs to the education system such as financial or enrolment data. The growing realization of the need for more information about the outputs of the system led to a burst of activity to generate such diagnostic data.

Early initiatives in this respect were typically designed as research studies building on the ideas and techniques pioneered in the international surveys of achievement referred to above. Typically, these evaluations were designed to explore in some detail the national pattern of strengths and weaknesses in particular subject areas. Generally based on a light sample of students, such approaches could, and did, use a wide range of often innovative assessment techniques to establish what kinds of achievements pupils of a given age were reaching in key curriculum areas. In some cases the monitoring was very detailed and provided extensive information about the processes students were using to undertake particular assessment tasks, as well as about the levels achieved.

Monitoring such as that conducted by the English Assessment of Performance Unit (APU) and the American National Assessment of Educational Performance (NAEP) project was typically not directly linked to particular education policies and was not designed to provide information at institutional level. The aim was rather to feed back into the education system, and into professional networks in particular, information about the strengths and weaknesses of various aspects of teaching in different subjects.

Such national monitoring based on the intensive study of a sample of the school population to establish prevailing levels of a wide range of knowledge and skills is still practised in many countries, such as New Zealand, and even Scotland. It has done a great deal to support the development of novel assessment approaches and tasks, as well as generating important information about the strengths and weaknesses of the relevant education system. The following description of the recent Dutch approach to national monitoring provides a good example of this approach:

> The aim of Dutch National Assessment is to get a clear picture of the current state of education in the country. Learner attainment at the end of certain periods, e.g. half-way and at the end of primary education, is used as one of the indicators to get information about the quality of the education system. National or system-wide assessment is explicitly *not* intended to make statements on the abilities of individual learners or on the quality of individual schools. Its focus is the educational system, for instance primary education. It addresses issues such as 'What do schools try to teach their pupils?', 'What do the children that participate in the system actually learn in education?', 'What specific skills and knowledge have they acquired?', 'What changes in educational offer and results have taken place over the years?' (European Network of Policy Makers for the Evaluation of Education Systems 2001: 4)

In other countries such as France, although the approach is to monitor the achievements of *all* children, rather than those of a representative sample, the purpose is still explicitly diagnostic. The data generated from national tests is fed back to teachers with the intention that they will use it to inform their teaching, as well as it being used to provide information for policy-makers concerning the strengths and weaknesses of the current system.

However, as the idea that the strengths and weaknesses of education systems as a whole could be measured in this way has gained credence, so the collection of information has become more sophisticated. It has also increasingly become associated with the notion that this kind of information can, and indeed should, be used for institutional improvement.

Thus we may chart over recent decades in very many countries, particularly in the Anglophone world, a move from research studies of the standards achieved by individual education systems towards national monitoring programmes, which involve assessments of the achievements of each student individually. Such national assessment programmes are typically used to provide data that can be used to judge the quality of particular institutions such as schools, as well as that of the education system as a whole. Often complemented by other features of 'the quality agenda' such as increasingly explicit requirements for institutions to undertake ongoing internal monitoring of standards, to set institutional targets and to submit to regular external inspections, the advent of national assessment programmes represents a profoundly important development.

Individual countries that have adopted the 'blanket testing' approach, vary considerably in the extent to which they are prepared to use the national test data as a lever to force institutions to 'play the game'. In many European countries, notably in Scandinavia, there is continuing resistance to the publication of institutional evaluation data, particularly in the form of student examination results. The information remains private to the institution. However, many other national systems have followed the example of England, in shifting from a diagnostically oriented, national monitoring system to a national assessment system explicitly designed to provide assessment data that is suited to being the currency of a market-based approach to educational consumption.

However, such national variations, important as they are, are still arguably less significant than the common features that they share. The most significant of these common beliefs is that of the desirability of more scientific forms of management based on the availability of performance data. Assessment for system control is now so deeply embedded in prevailing thinking that to abandon it seems as unthinkable as abandoning student assessment itself.

Activity 7.2

Consider a system of national assessment with which you are familiar. What is its prime purpose? What positive and negative effects of such a system can you identify and why?

Inspection – The Constant Gaze

Another manifestation of 'the quality agenda' in many countries has been the changing role of external inspection. Historically, most education systems, like other public services, have had a system of school inspection (Standaert 2001). Some of these systems have been designed to assess individual teachers – as, for example, in France. Others have had as their principal concern monitoring the quality of the education system as a whole – as, for example, in England. Many countries have had systems of local inspection as well. Inspectors have typically been important contributors to the formation of education policy at both national and local levels. But although their role in many education systems has been a 'high-stakes' one for individuals in that their judgements would influence career progression and also, often, posting decisions, this role has clearly been a personal one involving the decision of one human being about another.

The advent of 'the quality agenda' has typically changed this. It has replaced the humanistic judgements of tradition with a more managerialist approach in which the framework for judgement and many of the assessment tools used have been conceived and laid down from the centre. Traditional systems of inspection have been complemented by the operation of a national assessment system that prioritizes the results of *tests* as an indicator of either teacher or institutional quality. Again, the current inspection system in England provides a good example in this respect since it has been widely emulated in many other countries.

The Office for Standards in Education (OFSTED): An English case study

The advent of national assessment in England in 1988, brought with it national tests of achievement for all students at age 7, 11 and 14, to augment the existing system of public examinations at age 16 and 18, and more recently 17. The advent of these tests reflected the explicit intention to use the results as publicly available indicators of the quality of a given school. National assessment data has thus become increasingly 'high-stakes' for individual institutions, and indeed for Local Education Authorities too since these are also now the subject of league tables and subject to external inspection. The powerful impact on schools and LEAs of national test results is further reinforced by the results of regular external institutional inspections conducted by the Office for Standards in Education (OFSTED).

OFSTED is designed to provide for the comprehensive examination of all aspects of a school's life and achievements by a team of externally appointed, freelance inspectors. It largely replaces the previous system of Her Majesty's Inspectors (HMI) that was set up in the middle of the nineteenth century. Under this regime, nationally appointed professional inspectors were charged with inspecting schools on a sample basis in order to provide diagnostic insights concerning the strengths and weaknesses of different aspects of the system as a whole, rather than of individual institutions.

The impact of the combined policy initiatives of 'high-stakes' national assessment and a national system of institutional inspection, is significantly increased by virtue of the fact that the results of both exercises are published. This approach well-illustrates several of the key assumptions underpinning the arguments of this chapter concerning the advent of 'the quality agenda' as follows.

The 'panopticon'

The first of these arguments relates to the impact of surveillance. The awareness that an assessment is impending is likely to motivate those being assessed to 'put their house in order'. Just as students swot for exams, so institutions swot for inspections, even if the nature of the assessment dictates a slightly different approach to this swotting. We see here one of the most powerful characteristics of assessment, famously immortalized in Jeremy Bentham's vision of the 'panopticon' (Foucault 1977) in which individuals are potentially subject to constant scrutiny so that whether the gaze is on them or not, they will act as if it is. Not knowing when an inspection may come, but simply that it will, effectively creates a climate in which people behave all the time as if they are about to be inspected.

Providing for 'choice'

The second assumption underpinning the move towards national assessment and school inspection is that the availability of apparently objective data pertaining to institutional quality, will encourage consumers to be discriminating in their choice of institution. Parents are expected to examine this information and to use it to inform their choices. The awareness that parents will be doing this, and the financial and other consequences that follow, if a school becomes unpopular, are again a powerful step towards forcing institutions to toe the party-line as far as they are able.

Unfortunately, as we shall see in our discussions of league tables in the next chapter, institutions are not all equally well-placed to respond to such pressures, and no more are parents. The result tends to be, that as with students, many institutions become demoralized and increasingly incapable of disengaging themselves from a vicious downward spiral.

Market forces

A third associated assumption informing 'the quality agenda' is that competition, in itself, will stimulate higher levels of achievement whether this is for individuals or for institutions. As we explore at more length in Part Four of this book, there is little research evidence to support this assumption, and a great deal to suggest that this is not the best way to improve performance. There is little evidence to support the view that standards are rising in England as a result of recent policy initiatives, not least because where test data are used in a very high-stakes fashion, the pressure to 'teach the test' that is created makes it hard to interpret the data. Thus any rises in test performance that are documented are just as likely to be a result of the teaching of test technique.

In Texas, for example, where there was an apparently miraculous rise in high-stakes test scores in reading, this was subsequently found to be largely illusory because teaching test-technique and teaching to the test largely accounted for the rise (Tymms 2004). Likewise, a three-year study of mathematics teaching of nine-year-olds in New Jersey found that:

> Where teachers feel more pressure they respond with short-term test preparation and focus on more didactic instructional strategies. However, when they know more about State and National standards and have the opportunity to learn more they are inclined to use more enquiry-oriented approaches and integrate test preparation with regular instruction. (Firestone et al. 2004: 49)

Thus there must be considerable doubt that high-stakes national monitoring accurately reflects the quality of overall educational performance in any particular education system. As with IQ tests, such tests can only really be said to measure what they measure, rather than any more profound aspects of educational performance. For, as well as the significant 'washback' effect of such tests on classroom priorities, there is also, once again, the problem of 'the myth of measurement'. Many studies have exposed the wealth of technical difficulties involved in comparing standards over the course of time (Massey et al. 2003). Yet, as one of the world's leading statisticians has argued, without longitudinal data, causal inferences about the effects of educational systems must remain extremely limited and any attempt to make such inferences correspondingly unsound (Goldstein 2004).

The situation that has been briefly alluded to here – particularly as it has developed in England – represents what I have suggested is probably the most extreme tip of a much larger iceberg of developments which have characterized many countries in recent years. It is easy to be overly negative about such developments that clearly represent a tightening of central control. However, it is important to recognize that the generation of much more publicly available data about an educational institution than was available under traditional inspection systems, can be seen as a move towards greater transparency and, hence, accountability. The key question remains, however, whether greater central control at the price of professional autonomy, particularly when it is exercised through some kind of high-stakes assessment, will, in the long term, result in education systems that are more effective in preparing young people for the challenges of a new century, or whether this apparent transparency is itself a form of 'tyranny' in seeking to make what is inherently invisible, visible (Strathern 2000).

Activity 7.3

How far do you feel that the increased emphasis on inspection and institutional assessment has improved educational quality in recent years? What is likely to be the effect of this increasing assessment pressure on teachers and students?

Next Steps in 'The Quality Agenda'?

It has been the argument of this chapter that the advent of 'the quality agenda' has been associated with a shift towards greater central control based on the more or less punitive use of assessment data. Trusting professionals to be responsible for quality assurance has become increasingly unfashionable compared to the 1960s and 1970s. However, there are some signs that this situation is changing and that the pendulum is beginning to swing back towards recognizing the importance of individuals and institutions taking responsibility for standards through self-improvement.

There are now an increasing number of examples of institutional and professional self-evaluation providing the cornerstone of educational quality development in many countries and in different settings. The UK is fairly typical in this respect. In Scotland, for example, policy-makers have been quick to respond to school effectiveness research and the evidence that suggests a more modern approach to management may achieve much more in terms of both institutional development and the promotion of high-quality professional practice. Scotland is currently pursuing an approach to promoting quality that is centred on empowering those responsible for delivering it (Powell 2000).

In England too, perhaps in the light of growing evidence that the obsession with targets and external mechanisms of control is not resulting in the higher standards desired, there are some signs of similar developments. As a recent statement by Her Majesty's Chief Inspector of Schools intimated:

> After 12 years of OFSTED inspections, millions of pupils have benefited from improvements in the quality and standard of education in our schools. It is now time to build on the progress achieved over the last decade by moving to a lighter touch, but equally rigorous inspection regime with school self-evaluation at its heart. (Bell 2004)

Although this development may be informed by new educational thinking, it is also likely to be, in part at least, a reflection of the fact that three-quarters of the UK government targets for schools and hospitals in England have not been met (Kite 2002).

Thus in future, schools in England will be expected to use the multiple sources of data with which they are now provided to evaluate for themselves aspects of institutional quality and to generate suitable strategies for improvement. These sources of data include an enormous amount of pupil performance data, assessment data, classroom observation data, data from teaching plans, samples of pupils' work and learning outcomes, data relating to targets for achievement, data relating to collaboration and independence in learning, pupils' self-assessment data, pupil perceptions and staff perceptions (Elliott and Sammons 2000).

Thus, although assessment data are still central to the evaluative process, the assumptions underpinning *how* such data are to be used are beginning to change in recognition that fear and competition may not be the most effective way of getting the best out of students and teachers. Such recognition has been encouraged by the powerful impact of research on school improvement and school effectiveness that was a hallmark of evaluation research in the 1980s and 1990s that emphasized the key importance of institutional leadership and vision in raising standards (James 1998; Halsall 2001).

Moreover, as the combined technical and educational shortcomings of high-stakes assessment become increasingly well-documented, there are increasing calls for teacher assessment, externally moderated by means of shorter national tests, or even a return to a sample-based approach to national monitoring. If such tests were largely automatically marked as, for example, in Sweden, the costs would be comparatively modest but they would still enable the effective monitoring of national progress, and by providing a basis for assessments of equivalent standards across schools could continue to be used to motivate further improvement.

The parallels here with individual student assessment are most marked. They highlight the fundamental tension between the different assessment paradigms that form a key theme of this book. On the one hand, there is the *measurement* paradigm. This is embodied in inspections, targets and league tables, just as it is embodied in external summative examinations and tests for students. On the other hand, is the *learning* paradigm. For institutions this is embodied in notions of self-evaluation and professional responsibility just as for learners; it is associated with the logic behind reflection and review, self-assessment and action-planning.

The argument here is that in just the same way that self-assessment can empower learners – as we shall argue in Part Four – so institutional self-evaluation can empower professionals. The tension between the two approaches to 'the quality agenda' and the assumptions that underpin these two approaches, parallels the tensions surrounding different approaches to individual student assessment. This is the tension between the perceived value of rigorous summative, typically external, assessment versus the opportunity cost of such an approach to assessment in terms of the loss of the potential benefits of more empowering student self-assessment. This tension is summarized in Figure 7.3 below.

Summary

In this chapter, the aim has been to explore some of the key reasons for the rise of what I have termed 'the quality agenda', as this has been associated with a decline of trust in professionals and the rise of accountability mechanisms. We have examined politicians' growing love affair with assessment as the panacea for raising standards while increasing efficiency. It has been suggested that 'the quality agenda' is the product of a combination of many factors. These include the ever-increasing size of the educational budget and consequently

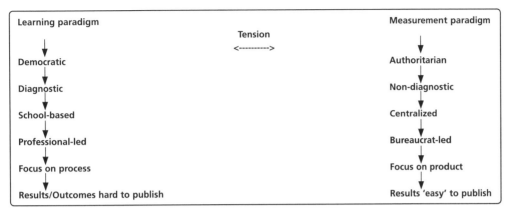

Figure 7.3 The Tension Between Measurement and Learning approaches to Assessment

greater demands for accountability and transparency; the pressure for international educational competitiveness and the steadily increasing sophistication of management practices at national and institutional levels.

Finally, we have briefly considered the capacity of these developments to raise standards and the signs that a new interest in professional reflection and development as a mechanism for educational improvement may mark the beginning of a change in the received orthodoxy of assessment-driven accountability. The pressure for greater accountability is unlikely to reduce. What may be changing, however, is the rather crude association of accountability with raising standards; the assumption that simply by piling on the pressure, individuals and institutions will be both motivated *and able*, continually to improve. It is increasingly apparent that this belief is naïve. While individuals may wish to hit targets, they may lack the knowledge and skill to be more effective. By contrast, strategies for institutional improvement that are centred on giving professionals themselves more responsibility are more likely to result in the necessary learning.

Thus, we may usefully revisit the distinction between assessment for curriculum and assessment for communication discussed in Chapter 1. The distinction made there between assessment for learning and assessment for 'measurement' is equally valid in the context of institutional assessment as it is in relation to student assessment. The fundamental differences between these two approaches to using assessment for institutional improvement emphasize the crucial importance of the questions posed in Chapter 1 concerning who to assess, what, how, when and, most importantly, why. It is apparent that any answer to these questions will require a choice to a greater or lesser extent between the 'measurement' and the 'learning' paradigm.

More generally, this argument also emphasizes the points made earlier about the process of evaluation and the fundamental importance of being clear about its purpose and the way in which the data generated from any evaluative activity are to be used. There can be no clearer illustration of the salience of this point than in the current fashion for indicators and league tables – one of the clearest manifestations of 'the quality agenda' – to which we now turn.

Key references

Daugherty, R. (1995) *National Curriculum Assessment: A review of policy 1987–1994*. London: Falmer Press.
James, M. (1998) *Using Assessment for School Improvement*. London: Heinemann.

Useful websites

http://www.teachernet.gov.uk/teachingandlearning/afl/PAT/

The Pupil Achievement Tracker (PAT) supports Assessment for Learning (AfL) by enabling schools to analyse pupil-level performance data against the results of pupils nationally. This powerful interactive tool includes value-added graphs, a target-setting tool and question-level functionality. The latest upgrade is available on the **Standards** website. See the **PAT page** for further information and read the **FAQs**.

http://www.teachernet.gov.uk/management/tools/performance/

- How well are we doing as a school?
- How well could we be doing?

The **national benchmark** information enables you to answer these questions. You can make comparisons with schools with similar levels of social deprivation (measured by free school meals eligibility), or with similar levels of prior attainment, or value-added (measured by the performance at the end of the previous key stage). Under the LEA Data Framework, schools can also expect to receive benchmark information about the other schools in their LEA. Other areas of TeacherNet (**www.teachernet.gov.uk**) touch on separate assessment questions (not necessarily related to the above):

http://www.ofsted.gov.uk/

This site contains a valuable collection of downloadable publications. You can now sign up for email alerts so that you get immediate notification of any additions to the site.

Indicators and League Tables

In her 2002 BBC Reith Lectures, Professor Onora O'Neill echoes many of the themes of the preceding chapter on 'the quality agenda'. She refers to a crisis of trust for which the remedy appears to be greater accountability. This accountability, she suggests,

> takes the form of detailed control. An unending stream of new legislation and regulation, memoranda and instructions, guidance and advice floods into public sector institutions … The new accountability culture aims at ever more perfect administrative control of institutional and professional life … They require detailed conformity to procedures and protocols, detailed record keeping and provision of information in specified formats and success in reaching targets. Detailed instructions regulate and prescribe the work and performance of health trusts and schools, of universities and research councils, of the police force and of social workers. And beyond the public sector, increasingly detailed legislative and regulatory requirements also bear on companies and the voluntary sector, on self-employed professionals and tradesmen … performance is monitored and subjected to quality control and quality assurance. The idea of audit has been exported from its original financial context to cover evermore-detailed scrutiny of non-financial processes and systems. Performance indicators are used to measure adequate and inadequate performance with supposed precision. Schools, hospitals and universities are then forejudged and funded by their rankings in league tables of performance indicators.

But as Onora O'Neill goes on to question, is the new culture of accountability and audit making professionals and institutions more accountable to the *public* or is it really greater accountability to regulators, to government, to funders, to legal standards, in short, to forms of central control? Although, in theory, the new culture of accountability makes professionals and institutions more accountable for good performance, in practice the real focus of performance indicators, she argues, is chosen for ease of measurement and control.

In what follows, then, we shall explore some of the central questions in this debate. These include:

- What are appropriate education indicators and how should they be chosen?
- What would constitute a good indicator?
- In what ways are indicators useful and, if so, for whom and why?
- What are some of their limitations and dangers?

In the last chapter, I sought to establish *why* evaluation has become such a key policy tool in recent years, particularly in the form of national assessment schemes. The choice of any particular indicator is likely to be significant both in the way that it reflects prevailing values and because it is likely to be instrumental in driving educational priorities in practice. Given the enormous significance of the particular indicators chosen, in this chapter we shall pursue a more extended discussion of the actual content that is chosen for assessment – that is of the issue of '*what* to assess'.

Here we find ourselves once again immersed in the fundamental tensions that surround assessment. Issues of validity and reliability are again pertinent as are questions relating to the fitness for purpose of the assessment and its 'washback effect' on the behaviour and priorities of individuals and institutions. Moreover, it is important to recognize the important distinction between *performance indicators*, which, as the term suggests, embody the notion of 'performativity' introduced in the last chapter; and *diagnostic indicators*. This latter term may be taken to refer to particular measures that have been chosen as diagnostics of aspects of systemic functioning. Although it is in the nature of indicators that they are chosen in order to be used for comparative purposes, such 'diagnostic indicators' are not 'high-stakes'. Their purpose is akin to that of national monitoring systems, namely, based on *the need to know*, rather than on a more or less explicit desire *to drive priorities*. We shall now consider this distinction in more detail.

Choosing Indicators

In one of the classic texts on the subject, Nuttall (1994) addressed the question of how the quality of educational systems can best be assessed and how indicators can be developed which are really useful for this task. Nuttall teases out the tension between the objective, scientific search for largely quantitative indicators of educational quality, and the overlay of political tensions that inevitably affect their use. He articulates one of the core arguments of this book in suggesting that, as with all assessments, the choice of what to measure, how, when, and, above all, why are decisions driven as much by values, assumptions and relative power, as they are by more technical judgements.

Thus decisions concerning what aspects of a given government service should be measured will reflect not only the desire to *know*, but also the intended use of the information. The purpose may be, for example, to demonstrate the apparent success of a particular policy. Equally, as discussed in Chapter 7, the goal may be to put pressure on institutions through the use of 'performance indicators' and the public 'naming and shaming' embodied in league tables of performance.

It is therefore vital to recognize that any indicator system embodies value judgements about what is meant by 'quality'; to recognize that what are defined as desirable outcomes for education or for any other state service, is, to a greater or lesser extent, the product of the democratic process. Thus indicators cannot in any sense be objective even if the mechanisms used for gathering the data that inform them appear to be so in that – as is often the case – these mechanisms are technically highly sophisticated.

Nuttall distinguishes two approaches to identifying what I refer to here as 'diagnostic indicators'. The first is derived from policy-makers' desire to know cause and effect relationships in order to help them anticipate the effects of potential policy initiatives. Complementary to this, is the more descriptive and typically more technical approach of modelling the component contributions of the educational process itself in terms of inputs, processes and outputs (Moskowitz and Stevens 2004).

Whatever their purpose, there is a simple list of principles for choosing such 'diagnostic indicators':

- Diagnostic indicators are suggestive of alternative actions rather than judgemental.
- The implicit model underlying the indicators is explicit and acknowledged.
- The criterion for the selection of indicators is clear and relates to the underlying model.
- As far as possible, individual indicators aim to be valid, reliable and useful.
- Comparisons are done as fairly as possible and in a variety of different ways, for example, with like groups, with self over time, and using dispersions and differences between subgroups as well as averages in order to avoid over-simplistic conclusions.
- The various consumers of the information generated are educated about its use.

In short 'diagnostic indicators' should be:

- both relevant and useful for policy-making by being timely, comprehensible and few in number;
- informed by relevant questions;
- oriented towards action;

- technically sound in terms of validity and reliability;
- feasible to measure at a reasonable cost.

The parallels with the desirable characteristics of evaluation procedures that were identified in Chapter 6 are clearly apparent here, reminding us that it is appropriate to see education indicators as just one particular manifestation of the more general practice of evaluation.

Using Indicators Diagnostically

The search for a valid and useful system of educational indicators to permit governments to diagnose the strengths and weaknesses of their own systems, and also to compare quality internationally, has proved to be a challenging one that has required a good deal of international collaboration. The OECD has undertaken one of the most sustained and substantial initiatives in the generation and use of 'diagnostic' indicator systems. The results of the OECD project are available as the 'Education at a Glance' series, which provides a continually updated comparative international snapshot of educational indicators.

The OECD's comprehensive approach to identifying indicators that can be used to compare aspects of particular education systems is laudable in its scope and technical rigour. In contrast, most 'performance indicators' are generated in a much less rigorous way yet they are far more 'high-stakes' in their influence on behaviour.

Activity 8.1

List what you consider to be the advantages and disadvantages of such national and international efforts to compare educational standards.

Performance Indicators

As the term implies, performance indicators are designed as a basis for judgement. The information generated, however, is rarely kept private. The close association of performance indicators with movements towards greater accountability, transparency and consumer choice, means that more often than not, the information generated is published. For the same reasons, this is often in the form of rankings, star ratings or some other form of comparison. Hence, even purportedly criterion-referenced assessments such as star ratings, rapidly become norm-referenced as institutions are compared with each other. Thus, so-called 'league tables' of institutional performance have become a ubiquitous feature of public life in recent years. Appearing in newspapers on a regular basis and consulted with enthusiasm by consumers of all kinds, league tables are used to inform individual choices about public services such as schools. They are also frequently the legitimation for policy decisions.

It is readily apparent that it is difficult to define the appropriate balance between what is arguably a necessary degree of monitoring of institutional quality or national standards given that some measure of such information is essential to effective quality assurance and control and the way in which these mechanisms frequently turn into the kind of crude drivers referred to by O'Neill above.

In English universities, for example, the advent of two national quality assurance exercises provide a powerful illustration of this tendency. One of these is the Research Assessment Exercise (RAE), which is conducted every few years by the Higher Education Funding Councils in the UK in order to inform the allocation of research funding to different institutions. Not surprisingly, the resultant grades are heavily used as the basis for national and international league tables and hence carry far more significance than that of money alone for individual institutions.

Similarly, the practice that prevailed for more than a decade of assessing teaching quality via periodic external reviews of individual subjects by the Quality Assurance Agency was also 'high-stakes' for institutions despite the fact that there was no direct impact on funding, because of their key role as an indicator in the construction of league tables. It is clear that these systems were designed, at least implicitly, as such indicator systems often are, to provide the basis for inter-institutional comparison. It was anticipated that such inter-institutional competition represented in 'league tables' of relative performance, together with an associated system of financial rewards and penalties in the case of the RAE, would drive up standards by encouraging institutions to try harder. It would also, importantly, provide a defensible basis for controversial funding decisions.

The effect of these exercises, not surprisingly, has indeed been to galvanize the English higher education system. League tables have enormous consequences for universities in terms of their popularity with potential students, their income and their perceived status. Not surprisingly, they have had huge impact on the priorities and processes of virtually all the institutions affected by them.

The same is true of the school inspection arrangements introduced with the Office for Standards in Education following the 1988 Education Act in England and Wales, which was referred to in the last chapter. This was an inspection system designed to provide public information for parents to inform their choice of school for their children. The creation of a comprehensive system of external inspection, according to an explicit template of indicators, the results of which were to be made public, was bound to have an enormous impact on the priorities and practices of schools. To the extent that this was the intention, it was very successful.

As is readily apparent, the impact of such exercises is typically a function of how 'high-stakes' they are in terms of the significance of the outcome for the institution in question.

Just as for individual students where 'high-stakes' assessments are the ones which determine their future life chances, so with institutions, 'high-stakes' assessments are the ones which affect their future funding, popularity and generally perceived success. Institutions that do not score well in terms of such 'high-stakes' indicators face a difficult and uncertain future.

The Advantages of Performance Indicators

Is the advent of 'performance indicators' a good thing? Certainly it is possible to identify many potentially positive effects from having them. Their advent heralded a new era of openness, providing consumers with the capacity for more-informed choice. They can be used diagnostically in identifying examples of outstanding excellence, which can inform work with other institutions to improve them in similar ways. Where the indicators are designed, as with pupil-assessment results, to indicate the 'value-added' by the institution in terms of the progress of an individual pupil, they are a valuable means of showing the effectiveness of a particular school. Indices of 'value-added' can diagnose an apparently high-performing institution in terms of its overall results, as one which is, in fact, coasting, relying on the quality of its pupil intake to get good results, and not doing as much as it might to improve the performance of its students. Equally, such measures of 'value-added' can help a school whose pupils are not high-fliers to demonstrate what may be a very significant improvement in their pupils' overall performance.

There is no doubt, too, that the advent of such external assessment exercises within institutions, either on a local or a national basis, has challenged institutions to examine themselves and to consider how they can improve. The advent of indicators and league tables has helped to discourage the complacency that can creep into institutions if there is little competition or pressure for accountability.

The Disadvantages of Performance Indicators

Against these potential benefits, however, it is important to consider the very significant dangers associated with the use of indicators, particularly where the results are used in league table form. Here are two examples of the kind of league tables typically published in English newspapers. One is an example of a schools' league table and one relates to universities' performance. Clearly the most obvious danger with league tables is that readers will not interpret the data intelligently in terms of context such as the catchment area of the school or its resources, but rather take the raw data at face value.

Let us look at a typical example in a little more detail. In the case of Figure 8.1 below the indicator in question is student dropout rate from British universities among those entering in the 2001/2 academic year. At first glance, this would seem to be a very objective measure with little scope for ambiguity. However, the range represented in the table from 1% at one extreme to 37% at the other, reflects huge differences in the type of student recruited to the different institutions and their consequent vulnerability to drop out through, for example,

Figure 8.1

	School	Location	Type	Score	
1	Town A School for Girls	London	M	100.00	466.00
2	County B School	Berkshire	G	100.00	444.92
3	C Academy	Liverpool	G	99.54	387.98
4	King School for Girls	Manchester	G	99.20	420.88
5	Archdeacon G CofE School	Lincoln	M	99.00	407.20
6	H School for Boys	Preston	B	98.30	479.52
7	St. J's College	Birmingham	M	98.00	509.60
8	N Grammar School for Girls	Birmingham	G	98.00	502.28
9	St. K Catholic School	London	M	97.33	467.05

Key to table
GCSE A* 58 points; **A** 52; **B** 46; **C** 40; **D** 34; **E** 28; **F** 22; **G** 16
M mixed **B** Boys **G** girls

(Example of league table for Comprehensive Schools; a separate list is produced for Grammar schools)

A comparison between norm-referenced and criterion referenced forms of assessment

Facet	Norm-refenced	Criterion-Referenced
1. Information provided about the learner	Summary in numerical or grade form of the general level of attainment in a broad area of learning.	Specific statements about what the learner knows and can do.
2. Information reported	Achievement in relation to other students in the group (marks or grades).	Description of the learner's competence (profile)
3. Domain of assessment	General prescribed subkect areas.	Specific learning outcomes.
4. Extent of assessment	Narrow range of examinable skills, mainly recall and application of knowledge.	Wide range of well-defined skills.
5. Educational purpose	Summative assessment achievement in relation to other learners.	Formative and summative assessment guides learner through the learning process.
6. Achievement levels measured	Wide range of levels with fine discrimination between students, not necessarily accurate.	Competence achieved or not yet achieved.
7. Moderation	After assessment by external examination and, possibly, sealing of marks.	Explicit standards Quality assurance through approval and accreditation mechanisms.
8. Most appropriate uses	Measuring general level of knowledge and understanding of a subject in order to rank or select student.	Determining competence based on set standards in specific roles or tasks.

	% Drop-Out	% Benchmark	% State Schools	% Benchmark	% Poorere Students	% Benchmark
University of A	1.3	3.5	57.6	76.8	11.3	17.3
University of B	2.1	3.0	55.4	77.2	11.0	17.2
University of C	2.3	6.4	68.3	80.1	15.1	20.4
University of D	2.5	5.6	72.8	79.9	16.9	21.0
University of E	3.1	6.9	83.0	88.3	37.0	29.4
University of F	3.2	5.0	66.1	79.3	18.0	19.8
University of G	3.3	6.2	79.7	83.8	16.8	23.9
University of H	3.4	4.5	63.8	78.9	13.7	20.0

Key: Universities are ranked by drop-out rate, the percentage of students entering in 20??/20?? who are not projected to complete their courses. Benchmark represents the expected figure for that institution.
State students is the percentage of university entrants from state schools in 20??/?? Bench mark is the expected percentage, based on univeristy profile.
Poorer students is the percentage of entrants from the lowest four social groups on the seven-point National Statistics Socio-Economic Classification in 20?? Benchmark is the expected percentage.
(Example of a league table for universities in the UK)

students not being able to cope financially or academically, as well as more general reasons such as ill-health. Thus, universities that are the most active in 'widening participation' are also likely to be those most vulnerable to being bottom of this particular league table even though they may be doing an excellent job in supporting their students. While the significance of such contextual information is readily accepted by the professionals involved, this is unlikely to diminish the impact of the raw data on a largely uninformed public.

This specific example illustrates the significant problems of accuracy and interpretation in many league tables. Thus, for example, the more general league tables of university 'quality' published by most national newspapers annually are full of, at best, misleading and frequently downright wrong information. This is because most of the tables aggregate incompatible measures, essentially adding 'apples and oranges'. The tables are typically formed from a set of rankings based on measures such as teaching quality, intake qualifications of students, employment success, research performance and facilities.

The fact that absolute figures are used effectively gives some variables much greater weight than others. For example, because the 'employment' figures have a relatively small dispersion over all institutions, changes to these have little effect on a university's overall position in the table, whereas dropout – with a larger dispersion – has a much greater impact. Atypical types of courses and students are normally not included, so that the tables tend to 'reward' universities with low staff–student ratios taking in 'standard' entrants with high A-level scores who complete in the expected time-scale. As such the tables provide a perverse incentive in relation to current UK government attempts to 'widen participation' to entrants from non-traditional social backgrounds. This example provides powerful testimony to the capacity for assessment to be used in ways that may run counter to its expressed intention. The primary purpose of newspaper league tables is to sell newspapers, not to inform. The accuracy of the information or any perverse effects is therefore of secondary importance at best.

The second example of a league table illustrated here reports the GCSE results of the 'top' schools nationwide (*The Guardian* 2005). Again, parents and students are likely to take the information at face value in their judgement of the quality of individual schools, taking little or no account of the differences in schools' intakes despite the fact that there is a strong correlation between a school's position in the league table and its geographic location. Top-scoring schools are much more likely to be located in leafy suburbs and other desirable residential areas, for example.

Moreover, recent research in England has found that head teachers use the 'per cent 5* A–C indicator' at GCSE (i.e. the number of students achieving a notional pass grade in the national examination at the end of compulsory schooling) as a key marketing tool, and strive by every means possible to raise their overall result.

> the need to focus on this measure [league tables] arises from its position as the headline figure, not because heads believe it provides an accurate measure of school performance … heads do not use this measure within their schools, instead they employ a range of measures to help improve student outcomes … (Wilson et al. 2005: 3)

The study found that value-added measures allow more accurate assessment of schools' performance but have little impact on heads' behaviour.

A similar and equally telling illustration in this respect is that of the indicator currently used for hospitals in England concerning the number of deaths per patients admitted. Where such an indicator is in play, the effect has in some cases been for hospitals to be deterred from admitting dangerously ill patients since the subsequent possible death of such patients might negatively impact on this performance indicator. This is clearly not the reason why such an indicator was chosen. It therefore provides a good example of the unanticipated, but often serious, consequences of choosing indicators that have not been thought through carefully.

In their pursuit of high scores and of meeting targets, institutions are likely to engage in the same kind of games playing as students seeking to spot particular exam questions and to swot up for them. 'Performance indicators' are therefore likely to exert a more or less perverse impact on the proper priorities of the institution. Whatever 'performance indicator' is in play, institutions will make efforts to maximize their scores for the purposes of assessment in relation to these indicators even if so doing has a negative impact on less overt aspects of quality. This is the fundamental argument against the 'performativity' culture that was discussed in the previous chapter.

Moreover, the effect of any public indicator system is likely to be divisive. Successful institutions will be able to celebrate their positive achievements and reap the associated rewards. However, those institutions that are less successful in terms of their league-table ranking, in either absolute or relative terms, are likely to feel increasingly demoralized and disheartened. Their poor placement in the ranking may also have financial consequences. As a result they may become both less able and less motivated to work towards improvement.

Activity 8.2

Given the difficulty of identifying and using indicators in a neutral way, how far do their benefits outweigh their dangers?

The Myth of Measurement Revisited

Undesirable as such a situation must be for those students, hospital patients, or other consumers who have little choice of institution, it might perhaps be tolerable if we could be sure that the data informing the league table's composition – 'the diagnostic indicators' – were accurate and valid. Sadly this must often not be the case as a now extensive body of expert international studies testifies (Vinokur 2005). For just as we saw in Chapter 2 in relation to the technical limitations of individual student assessment, so any process of institutional measurement must be subject to the same flaws. These potentially include:

- The measurement techniques chosen may be more or less valid.
- They may be more or less reliable.
- They are, by definition, arbitrary, the sample of aspects chosen as indicators working in favour of some institutions and against others.
- There will be game-playing and, perhaps, downright cheating.
- There will be mistakes made in collating the data.
- There will be bias that creeps in during the process of aggregating data which is perhaps both unanticipated and unremarked.

Thus league tables need to be taken with a very large pinch of salt for the weight they carry is often too heavy for the frail infrastructure that supports them to bear.

Some General Lessons

There are important issues here that are central to our understanding of the social consequences of assessment in all its forms.

- First, it is important to recognize that the particular criteria that form the basis of any assessment judgements cannot be value-free. Whatever dimensions are chosen for assessment, they will both reflect particular value decisions and favour some institutions or individuals more than others.

- Second, given the tendency for indicators and other assessments to focus on the easily measurable, this may well lead to the neglect of some more fundamental, but less easily measurable, qualities.
- Third, assessments impact on people. Evidence suggests, as we shall see in the next chapter, that this effect is particularly powerful when the result is negative. Although competition provides a spur, the fall-out for those who fare badly is often demoralization and reduced motivation resulting in the widening gap between high and low achievers in a climate of high-stakes testing that is now being widely documented. (Roderick and Engel 2001)

Boyle (2001) in a book entitled *The Tyranny of Numbers* summarizes the situation thus: 'because it is so hard to measure what is really important, governments and institutions try to pin down something else. They have to. But the consequences of pinning down the wrong thing can be severe.' Boyle identifies these 'counting paradoxes':

- You can count people but you can't count individuals.
- If you count the wrong thing you go backwards.
- Numbers replace trust but make measuring even more untrustworthy.
- The more we count, the less we understand.
- Measurements have a monstrous life of their own.
- When you count things, they get worse.
- The more sophisticated you are, the less you can measure.

In short, 'when we measure life, we reduce it' (*The Observer* 2001: 2).

Future Trends?

Recent years have seen a trend towards a rather different approach to the identification and use of performance indicators as part of more general developments within 'the quality agenda'. As I suggested in the previous chapter, these newer approaches are more professionally oriented and more formative. They represent a move away from external quality control exercised by means of inspection and targets, towards the provision of data which institutions are required to use to inform their own self-evaluation processes.

Such developments are apparent, for example, in English higher education where direct external inspection of teaching standards according to an externally derived template of standards – Subject Review – has been replaced by a much lighter touch 'Institutional Audit' (Ryan 2005). This new approach seeks only to assure the Higher Education Quality Assurance Agency that institutions' own quality assurance procedures are sufficiently rigorous. We might term this approach 'indirect inspection'. There has also been a significant fall in the burden of external accountability required of higher education institutions. A recent report from the Higher Education Funding Council suggests that the cost of accountability to higher education institutions has fallen from £250 million in 2000 to

£211 million in 2004 (PA Consulting 2004). However, it remains a very considerable sum of money in a climate of scarce educational resources.

What is being described here is an increasingly sophisticated approach to the diagnosis of institutional quality and development planning. As such the increasing trend to require institutions to engage in self-evaluation is potentially very fruitful. However, there continue to be dangers in such centrally imposed exercises even if they do allow greater autonomy to institutions in the way they are implemented. In England, the notion of 'earned autonomy' that has replaced more explicit inspection as the basis for quality assurance of university teaching, for example, still represents a 'panopticon' that constrains institutions' own creativity in this regard, and their professional capacity to address accountability issues in a way that is most appropriate for each institution's different mission (Ryan 2005).

A particular concern with regard to the more recent fashion for institutions to be required to use performance indicators, as the basis for development planning, is the assumption that any system of evaluation can be both formative and summative simultaneously. Even where the approach is one of 'indirect inspection' the still 'high-stakes' nature of externally imposed, accountability obligations of this kind is likely to lead to continued 'teaching the test' and game-playing, as well as a tendency to conform to externally defined notions of quality.

Perhaps the only truly formative approach to institutional quality assessment and development is one in which institutions are *trusted* to define and pursue their own quality agenda. Market forces are growing in significance in many countries at all levels of the education system as pressure for students to get good results becomes ever more intense, and students are increasingly paying high fee levels for both school and university. Arguably, this trend is likely to provide a sufficient mechanism to ensure the responsiveness of institutions to customer expectations concerning quality. Such consumer accountability, coupled with the deeply rooted moral accountability typical of most professionals who desire to give a good service to their clients, is arguably more than sufficient to counterbalance any loosening of the burden of bureaucratic accountability.

As O'Neill suggests, 'those who are called to account should give an account of what they have done and of their successes or failures to others who have sufficient time and experience to assess the evidence and report on it'. If indeed the day of the unaccountable professional is over, perhaps the era of 'intelligent accountability' provides a sensible compromise for the twenty-first century.

Summary

The considerable interest that has developed in recent years in the identification and use of education indicators is yet another reflection of the belief in assessment and evaluation devices to offer a rigorously scientific means of judging quality. Despite the fact that the scale of such activity has massively increased in preceding decades, this growth in the use of such tools has sadly not been accompanied by a corresponding development in the critical awareness needed to use such a powerful tool for good rather than ill (Vinokur 2005).

As has been discussed in this chapter, the consequence has been a tendency to focus on the readily measurable rather than the most valid indicators; to accept results at face value and to turn a blind eye to indicators that have a perverse effect. Indicators certainly have an important part to play in the analysis of institutional strengths and weaknesses, but they are a powerful tool that needs to be used sensitively and with due regard to professional consequences.

Key references

Fitzgibbon, C. (1996) *Monitoring Education: Indicators, quality and effectiveness*. London: Cassell.

Nuttall, D. L. (1994) 'Choosing Indicators' in Riley, K. and Nuttall, D. L. (eds) *Measuring Quality: Education indicators – United Kingdom and international perspectives*. London: Falmer Press.

Useful websites

http:// www.planning.ed.ac.uk/Pub/Tables.htm

This website from the University of Edinburgh provides an excellent set of materials on league tables and general commentary.

9 Assessing Professionals

Control or Empowerment?

In our exploration of 'the quality agenda', we have considered the way in which governments around the world have in recent years become increasingly enamoured of using educational assessment data as a policy tool. We have looked at national monitoring and assessment systems; developments in school inspection and other quality control devices that have combined to enmesh educational institutions in a network of external obligations that increasingly constrains what they do and how they do it. In the last chapter, we considered, in particular, the powerful influence of 'performance indicators' in this respect. It was suggested that some of the more extreme manifestations of performance indicators may be giving way to approaches to account-ability that provide for more local autonomy and, hence, indirect control of institutions.

Such moves embody understandings derived from the 'assessment for learning' paradigm and will be explored in more detail in Part Four where we look at this major new set of assessment perspectives in some detail. However, throughout this discussion, the tension between the 'measurement' and the 'learning' purposes of assessment has been a central theme of the analysis. Whether students learn better, teachers teach more productively, and institutions operate more effectively when challenged by 'high-stakes' external assessments or by 'low-stakes' formative feedback, has been a key question throughout this book.

In this chapter, we explore this issue in yet another assessment context: that of the assessment of professionals. Appraisal schemes, sometimes also termed staff reviews, are another important manifestation of the growth of 'the quality agenda'. In broad terms they also represent the desire to use assessment as a management tool in order to enhance quality. The advent of such schemes on a large-scale and systematic basis, represents a significant departure from historical practice when the role of any kind of assessment and feedback to inform most individuals' career progression was largely confined to the occasional pep-talk and the vagaries of the interview for a new job.

The rapid spread of appraisal both as a management tool and as a mechanism for professional learning, provides a very clear illustration of the tension between the 'measurement' and 'learning' approaches to assessment. It also provides perhaps the clearest expression that currently exists of an area of assessment activity in which the formative use of assessment has an explicit role and can carry considerable weight. Professional appraisal schemes, varied as they are in purpose, content and approach, nevertheless represent one of the first domains in which the validity of 'assessment for learning' has been both understood and recognized. As such, an analysis of this particular manifestation of assessment provides a useful link between the typical characteristics of 'the quality agenda' as we explored them in the previous chapters and the rationale of 'assessment for learning' which is the subject of Part Four that follows.

Multiple Subjectivities

Procedures for the regular and systematic assessment of staff are now ubiquitous in both industry and the professions. Such practices cover the full range of assessment purposes and practices that were identified in Chapter 1. At one extreme, they are designed to be formative, a key element in professional development; at the other, they can be highly summative, a 'high-stakes' assessment that will determine both career progression and financial reward. By the same token, the assessment of workers' performance evokes all the same questions as the assessment of students' performance – who is to be assessed, when, how and, above all, why.

Thus the discussion that follows will evoke many of the same themes that we have encountered in earlier chapters of this book – the need for clarity of purpose; the limitations of existing techniques; the emotional impact of assessment; and, above all, the scope for assessment to be either empowering or controlling. Like all assessment activity, staff appraisal has considerable potential for both good or ill for the individuals concerned, and it is subject to all the same concerns in relation to validity and reliability and fitness for purpose. In addition, the particularly individualist nature of such assessment provides perhaps the most powerful testimony available to the essentially social nature of educational assessment.

As I have argued elsewhere in this book, any kind of educational assessment is a human, rather than a scientific, activity, since it involves value-judgements not only at every stage of the process of deciding what is to be assessed, by whom, how and for what purpose, but above all in the making of the judgements that the assessment process requires. For even the most tightly specified criterion of performance can never be completely free from the relativities of human judgement. Thus, for example, an examiner using an apparently unambiguous criterion such as 'can swim 20 metres', in practice, will soon come up against the need for some interpretation of this statement in terms of, for example, factors such as the time taken, the temperature of the water and what constitutes 'swimming'.

When, by contrast, the performance in question is a complex professional skill such as teaching, such ambiguities are multiplied to such an extent that the assessment made can be 'objective' only to the extent that it comprises multiple subjectivities, involving the judgements of several different people, in different contexts and at different times. In the world of evaluation, this approach is known as 'triangulation', and is an important mechanism for reaching the best possible understanding of a particular phenomenon.

Indeed, we may usefully go a step further here and argue, with the phenomenologists, that there is no ultimate reality to be uncovered; that in social situations there are always multiple realities, each of which is valid for a particular individual. The task of the evaluator or the assessor is to reach a judgement concerning the largest area of common ground and, hence, which of these perspectives is the most valid.

But the problem does not stop with the range of values that assessors bring to the act of judgement. We must also take into account that performances themselves are ephemeral. If the athlete who can jump six feet on one day may not be able to do it the next, how much more is such variability likely when the context in question is not only highly charged emotionally, but relates to other individuals who are also just as subject to variability. Teaching class 10C on Monday morning is well-recognized to be a very different challenge from teaching them on Friday afternoon.

A Definition of Appraisal

So 'appraisal' is a good term to use for this particular activity. Not only does it avoid the excessively scientific baggage of more conventional forms of assessment, the very derivation of the word, from the Latin *pretium* meaning 'price' and *ad* meaning 'moving towards', emphasizes the managerial nature of the activity and the relationship between pay and performance that is central to the context of employment. 'Appraisal' then is more clearly than most other forms of assessment, an act of human judgement. As such it provides a useful reminder of some of the important general lessons about assessment contained in this book.

In view of the above, it is not surprising that the introduction of appraisal schemes has often been controversial. Nobody likes the experience of being judged, particularly when there is a lot at stake. Workers have tended to be suspicious of management's motives for introducing such schemes, particularly when the scheme's primary purpose is unclear. The two most common purposes are what we might term 'managerial' – for selection, promotion and the reward of merit; and 'professional development' – for enhancing skills and professionalism.

In terms of the latter, appraisal can lead to greater professional confidence and improved morale for both individuals and the institution as a whole as it may mean better professional relations and communication. It can be the means of targeting professional updating needs more accurately and in helping individuals with their career planning. It can even be helpful for individuals having problems who can be helped to face up to them and provided with suitable support. In short, it can encourage a culture of professional self- and peer-assessment that should, in turn, lead to better performance. As such, formative appraisal schemes are examples of assessment for learning, sharing the same core rationale as that for student self-assessment and other features of good formative assessment.

The other face of staff appraisal – to identify individuals who might one day be promoted; to decide 'performance-related pay' and to deal with incompetence – are clearly of a very different order and suggest the need for a quite different managerial process. Indeed these two purposes are often seen to be in opposition, or at best in tension. Despite this, there are many examples of schemes that have tried to be both and much has been written about whether any such scheme can work (Ko 2002; Chan 2006).

Activity 9.1

The 'managerial' and the 'professional' represent two rather different approaches to using assessment data in the context of evaluative activity that is concerned with teachers' professional development. Try to list the apparent advantages and disadvantages of both approaches and consider what policy conclusions this analysis leads you to.

Some Key Questions

Given that the distinction here is between schemes that are largely summative and schemes that are more formative, they typically involve different approaches. But whatever the purpose and the approach used, there are many questions that need to be answered. These questions echo the more general evaluation questions specified in Chapter 6. They include:

- Who should conduct the appraisal?
- Who should have access to the results of the appraisal?

- What criteria, and whose, should govern the appraisal process?
- What should constitute the content of the appraisal process?
- What measures of performance are appropriate?

If the purpose of the appraisal is formative, it needs as a minimum to be perceived by participants as fair, valid, comprehensive, transparent, practicable and useful – indeed all the elements of good formative assessment we discuss in more detail in Chapter 10. These requirements suggest others such as:

- There must be a climate of trust among staff and a sense of 'ownership' among all concerned.
- Those who will be the subject of appraisal should be involved in the design of the scheme.
- There must be clear, mutually agreed objectives for the procedure, together with a shared understanding of criteria and processes among all the parties involved.
- There must be a measure of triangulation in the formation of judgements.
- All the individuals involved need to receive training.
- There should be provision for monitoring and evaluation.
- Adequate resources need to be available.

Activity 9.2

Consider your experience of being an appraiser or of appraising someone else. What do you consider the most salient features of this experience?

The issues inherent in the appraisal of professional practice are thrown into particularly sharp focus by questions concerning *how* it should be done. While some schemes rely entirely on self-assessment and target-setting, and as such echo the rationale for lifelong learning more generally, others involve data gathered by one or more other people to inform the discussion.

Closely related to questions concerning 'how' the appraisal should be conducted are those concerning 'what' it should cover. Clearly some aspects of professional performance lend themselves more readily to assessment than others. Meeting a given sales target is relatively easy to determine. Deciding whether an individual fosters good relationships with subordinates is much more difficult. The inherent trade-off here between the reliability of the measures used and their degree of validity in fully encompassing the facets of a particular professional role, will be influenced, in this case, as in so many other aspects of assessment, by how 'high-stakes' the exercise is. For the most part, a significant element of 'soft data' will be acceptable, if the purpose is essentially formative.

However, the observation of professional performance is a particularly sensitive issue that deserves a little more discussion. We may use teachers as an example in this respect since classroom performance is a central aspect of their professional skill. Yet the issue of classroom observation has long been a particularly contentious aspect of appraisal schemes.

An early statement in the development of such appraisal schemes by English school inspectors opined 'without classroom observation, appraisal will lack real evidence of teaching skill and provide little that can be built upon to secure improvement' (HMI 1985). There is clearly a good deal of logic in this statement. Whether the intention of the appraisal is formative or summative, any judgement of teacher performance that does not include their activities in the classroom must be very limited. This is an issue of validity. However, precisely how such observation should be done and by whom, raises a number of important questions.

First, there are issues of how much observation is required and on how many different occasions to provide sufficiently reliable data. Second, there is the question of what is to be observed? Teaching style? Student behaviour and engagement? To what extent are these dimensions really valid indicators of teaching quality? What is a strength in the performance of one teacher may be a weakness in another depending on their overall style and the context in which they are working. Moreover, who the observer is – peer or senior colleague, perceived friend or foe – as well as how they behave – will undoubtedly influence both the teacher's performance and the observer's judgements. Anyone who has been through an inspector's visit or a visit from a tutor while undergoing teacher-training, knows only too well how the presence of even the friendliest observer can alter the dynamics of a classroom.

Moreover, there is little agreement as to what constitutes many of the elements of effective teaching and even less about what criteria should be used to assess it in practice. Although there are clearly many aspects of effective teaching that can be agreed upon – classroom control, well-organized lessons, interesting content, good working relations with students and so on – there are also less definable and observable elements that may make all the difference for an individual student's motivation or understanding. Such inspirational qualities may well not be definable in a conventional checklist of behaviours and may even accompany quite a weak performance in conventional skills.

This point is well-demonstrated by the illustration below which is an extract from one particular classroom observation schedule for the assessment of a teacher's classroom performance (Figure 9.1). It will be immediately apparent that the schedule makes a number of assumptions about what constitutes good classroom practice. The schedule also leaves little room for interpretation or qualification, requiring an instant, categoric judgement from the observer. This 'tick in the box' approach is extremely behaviourist in dwelling on what the teacher is perceived to *do*, rather than on the apparent impact of her actions. We may surmise that it is designed such that the assessment involved will appear as objective as possible, based on observable behaviour.

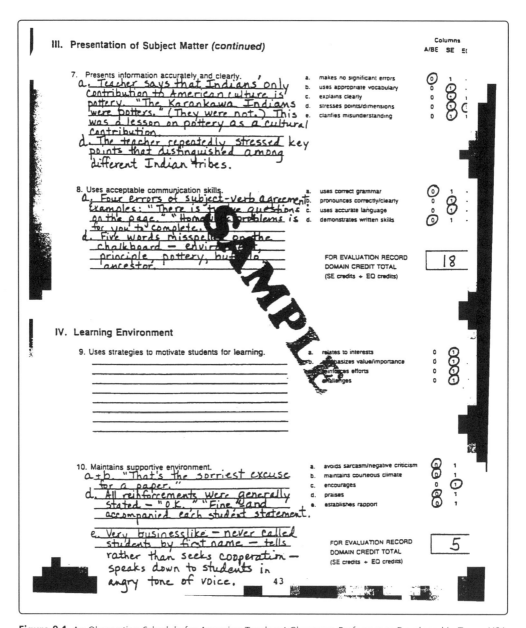

Figure 9.1 An Observation Schedule for Assessing Teachers' Classroom Performance Developed in Texas, USA

Activity 9.3

Consider the factors that you feel ought to be included in any assessment of a teacher's professional competence. How might these be fairly judged?

The extent to which the assessment is a valid representation of the teacher's overall quality, must be open to doubt. Still more open to doubt is the value of the schedule for developmental purposes. It is conceivable that the results of such an observation could be used constructively for diagnostic purposes as part of a more extensive discussion of classroom performance. However, the emphasis on reliability and quantification suggests a more summative purpose. This is in fact the case. The schedule was used as part of a scheme to determine which teachers in a school should receive merit payments for their outstanding performance. Since there were only a limited number of such payments available in any one school, rather than encouraging healthy competition, the essentially norm-referenced nature of the exercise proved deeply divisive. In the event, many teachers rejected the merit payments in solidarity with their less fortunate colleagues.

I have quoted this example at some length because it illustrates several important aspects of appraisal schemes. These are the issues of validity, 'washback effect' and fitness for purpose. I have suggested that attempts to assess teachers' classroom performance (and, by implication, that of any other complex performance or professional skill), on the basis of observable behaviours alone, is unlikely to be a very valid representation of the qualities in question. Clearly there is a place for such data as part of a broader picture of job performance, but it needs to be used interpretatively, rather than as an apparently objective score. The latter approach is, at best, unhelpful; at worst, misleading.

Even more serious, arguably, is the missed opportunity for professional development if results are used competitively rather than diagnostically. In addition, as happened in this example, far from motivating teachers to try harder to gain the extrinsic reward, this professional assessment scheme had the opposite effect. It demoralized the many teachers who inevitably could not win and eroded the very team spirit that is widely agreed to be a key element of effective schools.

In short, failure to consider adequately the 'fitness for purpose' of the assessment techniques chosen in terms of their potential 'washback' effect and overall utility, resulted in both a great deal of wasted effort, significant missed opportunities for real improvement and a great deal of personal unhappiness.

Unfortunately, this is not an isolated example. Indeed, it is one of the key messages of this book that the world of assessment – in whatever context it is practised – is more often than not characterized by these three evils of wasted effort, significant missed opportunities for real improvement and a great deal of personal unhappiness. All of us – probably without a moment's hesitation – can recall assessment events in our lives – a school exam perhaps, or even a more routine piece of homework – in which the careless use of assessment had effects that were deeply upsetting and surprisingly enduring.

> ### Activity 9.4
>
> Consider two occasions when you have been judged in relation to a particular performance, one when you were successful and one when you were not. How did you feel?

We return to the important and neglected issue of the emotional impact of assessment in Part Four. However, in the particular context for assessment under discussion here – namely the huge growth of professional assessment schemes in recent years – the salience of the 'three evils' identified above is compelling. For although appraisal schemes have typically become rather more sophisticated and professional in recent years, the enthusiasm for 'performance management' approaches shows little sign of abating. The use of this term is in itself significant, embodying as it does, two of the key assumptions underpinning 'the quality agenda'.

Performance Management

Some protagonists of performance management schemes argue for the inclusion of student performance as an indicator of teaching quality. But, while this may seem desirable in theory, no reader of this book can fail readily to see the many pitfalls and potential injustices that this would lead to, as well as potentially very undesirable 'washback effects'. These are well-illustrated in the classic 'payment by results' system of nineteenth-century England which was referred to in Chapter 1.

A major study of the recently introduced scheme in England for performance-related pay based on 'performance threshold assessment' found several worrying outcomes of the scheme. First, it had a significant and largely negative emotional impact on teachers. For the many for whom the oppressive 'standards' agenda had already created high levels of alienation and anger, this was further reinforced. Second, and perhaps even more important, certainly in terms of the argument of this book, was the finding that rather than relationships with students forming the basis of teaching and learning, staff were found to be becoming increasingly focused on student progress data and on individual students as helping or hindering the achievement of their targets. The increasing instrumentalism of teachers was in turn creating a similar reaction among students which found expression in discipline problems and disaffection.

Third, as in other countries where such approaches have been tried, it was found that assembling the necessary evidence base diverted teachers' time and attention from the core business of teaching. Thus, 'Whatever its real intentions, failure to gauge how the policy would be interpreted by teachers, within a specific political and historic context, merely served to further disillusion, not "motivate" them' (Mahoney et al. 2004: 453).

Rather than heeding this evidence, however, the UK government plans to go further as far as teachers in England are concerned by requiring that schools provide individual student performance data to parents on request as a means of identifying and 'weeding out' poor teachers. Such a development can only exacerbate the effects identified above, effects that are particularly regrettable in the light of the finding that a more developmentally oriented system of performance management linked with opportunities for further professional learning was welcomed by teachers and managers alike and that the 'Chartered Teacher' initiative in neighbouring Scotland which did have this latter rationale, had been much more positive in its impact (Menter et al. 2004).

Figure 9.2 provides an extract from one school's translation of this policy. It shows clearly the two different agendas of using the review cycle for professional development on the one hand and as the basis for making judgements in relation to extra payment on the other. It also provides an example of how seriously the business of professional appraisal is now taken by all those involved – the professionals themselves, managers and policy-makers. This is because such procedures can represent a unique opportunity for the individual to gain valuable feedback on their strengths and weaknesses; an opportunity for individuals to explore potential career opportunities and development needs with a senior colleague in a realistic and constructive way.

At their best, such procedures have a clear rationale; involve several different sources of assessment data and are both carefully prepared for and equally carefully followed up. But however well prepared for, some encounters will fall well short of this ideal simply as a result of the limitations of individuals and the pressures of daily life – the all too human realities of all assessment encounters.

Fundamental to the issue of the assessment of professionals is the underpinning evidence that now exists concerning the factors that are likely to result in improved performance. Accountability mechanisms can be simply about ensuring a given standard of performance; or they can be a mechanism to encourage professional growth and improvement. Which emphasis is chosen in the design of any particular appraisal scheme will depend to a large extent on the view taken of the teacher's role.

The issues concerning fitness for purpose are particularly important in this context and reinforce the general argument concerning the importance of a high degree of assessment literacy in this respect. Equally important is that the design of any such scheme should be informed by the findings of systematic evaluation procedures concerning the strengths and weaknesses of particular approaches such as that of Wragg et al. (1996), who identified a number of key features that need to be addressed if appraisal is to be fruitful in developing the quality of teachers' practice.

3. These may be summarized as follows:
   - To professionally challenge all staff within a supportive framework;
   - to recognise successes and achievements;
   - To support the achievement of whole school and departmental targets;
   - To enable the evaluation of benefits and outcomes;
   - To support the professional development of individual staff;
   - To enable managers to support their departments.
4. The performance management scheme will operate with fairness.
5. There will be equality of opportunity whereby all teachers are encouraged and supported through agreed objectives, access to relevant professional development and assessment of their performance.

The Annual Performance Management Cycle
6. The process will establish that teachers are meeting all reasonable expectations in respect of the discharge of their responsibilities. It will involve a three-stage annual review process.

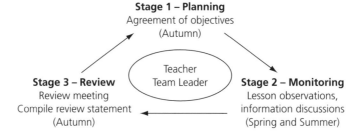

Stage 1 – Planning
Agreement of objectives
(Autumn)

Teacher
Team Leader

Stage 3 – Review
Review meeting
Compile review statement
(Autumn)

Stage 2 – Monitoring
Lesson observations,
information discussions
(Spring and Summer)

Stage 3 – Reviewing Performance
17. There will be an annual review meeting between the teacher and the team leader which will use the recorded objectives as a focus to discuss achievements and to identify any development needs, including the proposed action, resources available within the school budget, development plan and professional development policy, and the support to be provided.
18. A written review statement will be prepared by the team leader at the review meeting recording the main points made and the conclusions reached, including any identified development needs in a separate annex (but forming part of) the review statement. If it is not possible to complete the statement at the review meeting, it must be prepared by the team leader within 10 working days of the meeting. The teacher will be provided with a copy and may, within 10 working days of first having access to the copy, add to it comments in writing. Once written, the team leader will give the teacher a copy of the statement. The teacher may, within 10 working days of first having access to the statement, add to it comments in writing.
19. There will only be two copies of the review statement – one held by the teacher and another held by the head on a central file, to which the team leader or governors responsible for making decisions regarding pay could request access.

Figure 9.2 School Performance Management Policy

Summary

The development of the widespread practice of staff review or appraisal in recent years provides telling illustration of the capacity for assessment practices to serve very different purposes. In a way that is not yet widely understood in relation to student assessment, the choice between managerialist and developmental approaches to staff appraisal is increasingly widely recognized in practice, as well as in the relevant research literature. Equally the lessons to be derived from recent work on assessment for learning are highly relevant in the context of appraisal.

Unfortunately, this has not prevented the development and use of some very negative practices in which managers seek to use the appraisal procedure to pursue both formative and summative goals simultaneously (Hartley and Broadfoot 1986). Moreover, there are still many gaps in our collective understanding about how best to manage such schemes; how they impact on individuals who are subject to them and how best to provide for quality assurance.

In short, the 'who', 'what', 'how' and 'why' questions identified in Chapter 1 are clearly equally pertinent in relation to appraisal schemes. Professionals are expensive; their skills and attitudes are critically important to the success of the enterprise in question and they are typically very committed. Getting the use of assessment to monitor and, hopefully, develop their skills right is therefore an issue that is very high-stakes indeed. It is thus remarkable how often the practices used are based on assumptions about 'what works', rather than on the available evidence. As I suggested earlier in this book, one of the important reasons for this is simply a widespread lack of 'assessment literacy' – knowledge and understanding about assessment, the strengths and weaknesses of various techniques and, hence, their likely fitness for the task in hand and subsequent impact.

There is another explanation, however, which has also been referred to earlier in this book. This is the value of assessment as a political device, either to demonstrate that strong action is being taken, say about 'standards' – in this case of teachers' performance – or to provide the necessary legitimacy for a particular policy such as rewarding the few, rather than the many, because it is cheaper. The point is reiterated here simply to reinforce the general argument that the many shortcomings in the way in which educational and other forms of assessment are used in today's society which I have drawn attention to in this book, are only partly the result of ignorance or carelessness. In many cases, they are the direct result of assessment being used more or less cynically as a powerful way of providing pseudo-scientific legitimation for potentially unpopular policies or decisions; in short, the use of assessment as a technique of power.

Indeed, whatever the reasons behind the initiation and design of particular assessment practices, the one constant that is true of all of them is power. This power will vary in strength depending on a range of factors and it may be used for good, as well as for ill, as we explore in Part Four. The central theme of this book, however, is the critical importance of recognizing this, given the defining impact of assessment on contemporary society.

Key references

Hartley, L. and Broadfoot, P. (1986) 'Assessing Teacher Performance'. *Journal of Education Policy* Volume 3, Number 1, pp. 39–45.

Mahoney, P., Menter, I. and Hextall, I. (2004) 'The Emotional Impact of Performance-Related Pay on Teachers in England'. *British Educational Research Journal* Volume 30, Number 3, pp. 435–57.

Menter, I., Mahoney, P. and Hextall, I. (2004) 'Ne'er the Twain Shall Meet? 'Modernising the teaching profession in Scotland and England'. *Journal of Education Policy* Volume 19, pp. 195–214.

Useful websites

http://www.teachernet.gov.uk/management/payandperformance/performancemanagement/

The site explains what's involved in the new performance management arrangements introduced in Autumn 2006. Its explicit aim is to help teachers get the most out of performance management and ensure that it's carried out fairly and effectively.

Part Four
ASSESSMENT FOR LEARNING

The Emerging Evidence

From Summative to Formative

As previous chapters in this book have made clear, most of the history of educational assessment has been concerned with the development and use of devices for measuring student achievement for purposes of communication, whether these purposes be the certification of achievement, the selection of individuals or the evaluation of a particular initiative or programme. More recently, the same set of perspectives has been extended into the assessment of teacher quality, institutional quality and the quality of substantial parts of the education system itself such as school performance or higher-education teaching.

As was made clear in the chapter on evaluation, however, all assessment has the potential to be formative as well as, or instead of, summative; to be developmental in its impact, rather than simply being concerned with some aspect of the *communication* of information, contributing instead directly to the *learning* of either individuals or institutions. In what follows, we shall explore some of the implications of these developments both in terms of the emerging research evidence and how it is being used. The discussion will focus particularly on assessment for learning with regard to students rather than institutions since this is the area in which, so far, the most radical developments have been taking place.

It is only relatively recently that the potential of assessment directly to support learning has begun to come under the spotlight as it is increasingly being recognized that 'raising standards involves focusing beyond *what* children learn, to *how* they learn and *how* teachers intervene in this process' (McGuiness 1999). Longstanding work by psychologists in the field of learning has started to inform and be linked to more pragmatically driven work by educationists trying out particular techniques in the classroom. Such work has begun to offer some powerful insights into radically new ways of using assessment *for learning* rather than *of learning* – what has hitherto been referred to, in this book, as 'assessment for curriculum'. In this part of the book, we shall explore the powerful evidence underpinning these new assessment perspectives and practices and some of the practical ways in which they are now being implemented. Our discussion will be framed by three overarching questions:

- What role can assessment play in promoting learning whether of individuals or of institutions?
- How can assessment be used as an instrument of empowerment?
- What is the relative importance of assessment as compared to other interventions in promoting learning and developing quality?

To begin to answer these questions we need first to develop the distinction between assessment *of* learning and assessment *for* learning in terms of the distinction between formative and summative assessment that was briefly referred to in Chapter 1 since these terms are now often used interchangeably in the educational community. Assessment *of* learning refers to the very general *communication* function of assessment, whereas assessment *for* learning refers to what I termed earlier assessment as *curriculum*. The distinction between summative and formative assessment, while evoking many of the same distinctions, is also rather more specific, implying a particular purpose and assessment approach.

We may define summative assessment as assessment that takes place at particular times when achievement is to be reported, typically, against the same explicit criteria. It is likely to emphasize reliability and often to involve some kind of moderation or quality-assurance procedure. Essentially its purpose is to sum up the progress of an individual in relation to some given criterion. The key characteristics of summative assessment are summarized below:

- It takes place at certain intervals when achievement is reported.
- It relates to progression in learning compared against public criteria.
- Results for different students can be combined since they share the same criteria.
- It requires methods that are as reliable as possible without endangering validity.

- It involves quality-assurance procedures.
- It should be based on evidence from the full range of learning goals.

By contrast, formative assessment has to be planned as an integral part of teaching and is orientated to supporting progression in learning. It may be either criterion-referenced or student-referenced and its purpose is to lead to action that will support further learning and attainment. It is a process used by teachers and students to recognize and respond to learning in order to enhance it and identify next steps. Another definition suggests that 'formative assessment refers to all those activities undertaken by teachers and by the students in assessing themselves, which provide information to be used as feedback to modify the teaching and learning activities in which they are engaged'. Such assessment becomes 'formative assessment when the evidence *is actually used*, to adapt teaching to meet students' learning needs (Black and Wiliam 1998).

Thus formative assessment is typically conducted in the learning setting but is not synonymous with teacher or continuous assessment. At its heart it must be a dynamic process that has a real effect on learning having been planned and integrated into the teaching/learning process itself. Used properly, it gives students opportunities to practise skills and to consolidate learning, and provides opportunities for reinforcement as well as guiding further instructional and learning activities. In the form of corrective feedback it can help students to develop self-monitoring skills and to feel a sense of achievement. Truly formative assessment involves students themselves as partners in the learning process, assessing their own performance and deciding their next steps, as well as being empowered with the knowledge of how best to take those next steps. Some examples of how this is currently being done are discussed in Chapter 11.

To fully understand the potential and significance of good formative assessment to enhance learning, it is necessary to examine the nature of learning itself in a little more detail. This will enable us to make the connections between the key factors influencing learning and how these are provided for in formative assessment – assessment *for* learning or even assessment *as* learning – 'the process of seeking and interpreting evidence for use by learners and their teachers to decide where the learners are in their learning, where they need to go and how best to get there' (Assessment Reform Group 2002).

Learning

Learning is often taken to be synonymous with the intellectual or cognitive domain defined long ago by Bloom, for example, in terms of the hierarchy of increasingly sophisticated skills of knowledge, understanding, reasoning, analysis, synthesis and judgement. The design of many curricula has been dominated by this taxonomy. Much less influential, have been Bloom's attempts to capture what he recognized as other key facets of learning including what he referred to as 'the affective domain'. This is perhaps not surprising in view of the difficulties involved in defining in any operational sense what this domain comprises.

However, it is a sad reflection of how little explicit attention is typically given within the learning process to the affective domain, despite the fact that it is this domain, at least as much if not more than the cognitive, that influences an individual's level of engagement and success in the learning process. Moreover, as I argued earlier in this book, while assessment has a very important role to play in supporting learning in the cognitive domain, it has an even more powerful capacity to help or hinder learning in terms of the latter's affective dimensions.

Activity 10.1

Consider an activity that you have chosen to learn such as a sport or a hobby. How do your feelings about this activity differ from those you have typically experienced in a formal educational setting such as school or university?

A recent study has summarized the most important of these dimensions as follows:

1 *Self-esteem* – how one values oneself as a person and as a learner.
2 *Self-efficacy* – how capable one feels in succeeding in a learning task.
3 *Self-regulation* – the capacity to evaluate one's own work and to make choices about what to do next.
4 *Goal orientation* – whether one's goal is to learn in order to understand or to perform well on a test.
5 *Interest* – the pleasure from an engagement with learning.
6 *Effort* – how much one is prepared to try and persevere.
7 *Locus of control* – how much one feels in control of learning as opposed to it being directed by others.
8 *Sense of self as a learner* – how confident one feels at being able to learn from the classroom experiences provided. (Harlen and Deakin-Crick 2003)

These, rarely articulated, factors play a key role in classroom encounters. While other important contextual factors such as the institutional ethos, the student's own cultural and family background, the prevailing peer culture, the nature of teaching and the substance of the curriculum will each have a part to play in helping or hindering learning, there is clear evidence that it is feelings and emotions, that fundamentally help or hinder the extent and quality of learner engagement.

Clearly, individual characteristics in terms of the above dimensions are more or less fixed. Interest, for example, is likely to be a fairly fluid characteristic depending on a number of factors in play both inside and outside the learning setting. My interest in learning to ski may be a long-term and intense one, but still be substantially diminished on a particular occasion if the teacher's approach is dull or the snow is not good. Effort is likely to be similarly affected. By contrast, sense of self as a learner is more likely to be a long-term feature of an individual's persona, as difficult to alter as it is significant.

A less generic way of describing the key features of an individual's learning persona is provided in a recent attempt to define through empirical analysis those attitudes and dispositions that distinguish different types of learner (Deakin-Crick et al. 2004). Based on the concept of 'learning power' it seeks to define the mix of psychological dispositions, personal experience and social relations, which together constitute the forces that will influence learning in any given situation. In its own way, this 'mapping' of the 'learning genome' is as potentially profound as that of the human genome itself.

The five key dimensions of 'learning power' have been identified as 'learnability', 'dependence', 'creativity', 'learning relationships' and 'strategic awareness'.

- 'Learnability' is associated with an enthusiastic, critically curious approach to learning involving meaning-making, as opposed to 'stuckness', where the learner is a passive and uninterested participant.
- The resilient learner persists and is self-reliant in the face of difficulties, as opposed to the fragile and dependent learners who give up easily.
- The creative learner is willing to take risks and to allow their intuitive thinking process to come into play, as opposed to those who prefer to play it safe and stick to well-known rules.
- 'Learning relationships' involve an active engagement with other learners and with the community, as opposed to isolation.
- 'Strategic awareness' involves being able to articulate thoughts about one's own learning, as opposed to not feeling a sense of ownership of the process.

These dimensions make clear the complex interrelationship between intellectual activities and growth on the one hand and the feelings, emotions and drive that shape the quality of that intellectual engagement on the other, that constitute the petrol in the engine.

The key point here is not which of the many attempts to define the key elements of learning is most accurate. Rather, it is to demonstrate how important it is to appreciate the many and varied factors at work in the learning process; to understand the salience of these and to devise teaching techniques that take this full range of factors into account. Critical in this latter respect is assessment since, as I have argued, this is the dimension of the learning relationship that carries the greatest emotional charge. Also because, by the same token, it has the greatest potential to help individuals develop into better learners.

In a trenchant expression of this argument, Abbot puts the point thus: 'learning has to do with a hunger to make sense of something. The whole brain including the emotions, has to be engaged. If you separate emotion from intellect you court disaster' (Abbott 1998: 4).

The diagram below (Figure 10.1) represents this relationship in terms of the DNA double helix, nicely capturing its fundamental importance to learning.

These findings appear to hold true despite significant variations in the organization, delivery and cultural setting of education in different countries. Comparative research has shown that, on the one hand, learning is a social phenomenon. How teachers approach their professional task, the nature of the classrooms in which they operate, the curriculum goals they pursue and the nature of the social relationships that they construct with their students are all demonstrably social constructs. Likewise, how individuals learn, whether they are motivated to engage with the learning opportunities presented at any given time and how successful they are in making progress, are all powerfully affected by the social and cultural context. Cognitive and affective domains, personal qualities and relationships are all crucial to effective learning. Indeed there appear to be five constants that underpin effective teaching and learning (Osborn et al. 2003; Hufton et al. 2006):

- creating a climate of mutual respect and fairness;
- providing opportunity for active learning;
- having a sense of humour;
- making learning interesting;
- explaining well.

These findings are confirmed by a study of young adolescents in the United States. Here again students felt that the level of their engagement and motivation was significantly affected by:

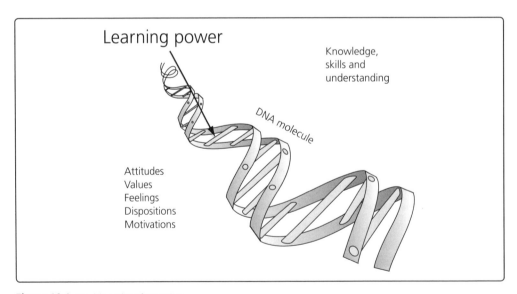

Figure 10.1 Double Helix of Learning

Source: McGettrick 2002

- the perception of the teacher as being supportive;
- encouragement to learn interactively and collaboratively;
- the creation of a climate of mutual respect;
- encouragement and the downplaying of competition;
- flow.

In short, the study argues that the level of students' motivation and engagement is significantly affected: 'when students believe they are encouraged to know, interact with and help classmates during lessons; when they view their classroom as one where students and their ideas are respected and not belittled; when students perceive their teachers as understanding and supportive; and when they feel their teacher does not publicly identify students' relative performance' (Ryan and Patrick 2001: 456).

There is also evidence that teachers too perceive these dimensions as crucial for student motivation, not least the degree to which assessment is being used to support learning rather than competition. The interrelationship between these various factors is summarized in Figure 10.2.

In the next section, we shall look in a little more detail at some of these key factors that affect learning and how these relate to new assessment thinking, thus linking learning and assessment.

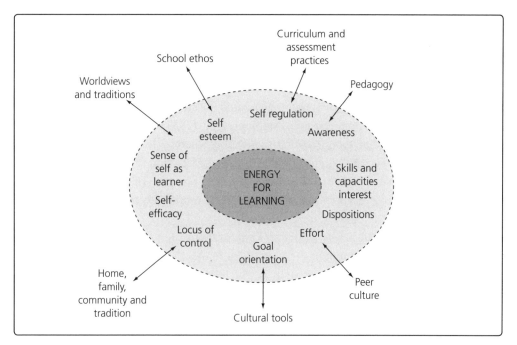

Figure 10.2

Source: Deakin-Crick (2004) ELLI Project Final Report

Motivation, Effort and Goal Orientation

There is a great deal of research concerning the nature and impact of motivation on student learning (Boekaerts 2002). Perhaps the most striking thing about this research is how little impact it has had on day-to-day practice in education. If it is true, as the old proverb suggests, that 'you can take a horse to water but you can't make it drink', it is equally true that unless a student is motivated to study and to learn, it is unlikely that all the teacher's skills will make this happen. Yet the issue of motivation attracts relatively little prominence in educational debates compared with, for example, teaching strategies or curriculum design. Though school reports with 'needs to try harder' are all too plentiful, rarely are such exhortations accompanied by an attempt to explore *why* the student is not motivated. If students are 'careless', 'lazy', 'easily distracted' or 'lack interest' this is a symptom of lack of engagement, rather than an explanation per se.

Activity 10.2

If you still have a school report, have a look at some of the entries. Try to remember what your reaction was when you first received these comments. Did they help you to improve, do you think?

By the same token, we are all familiar with individuals who really struggle with formal education but find learning effortless when it concerns details of their favourite football team or learning to play complex computer games. Unlocking the door to such 'energy for learning' would release untold capacity for increased success into the education system.

Moreover, the type of motivation that is generated is also very important. In her comprehensive review of motivation research, McMenniman (1989) argues the importance of developing *intrinsic* rather than *extrinsic* motivation whereby learners are stimulated to want to engage in an activity because of the intrinsic satisfaction they gain from it, rather than from the promise of high marks or other extrinsic rewards. The latter she argues will lead to, so-called, surface learning whereas the former is more likely to lead to deep learning – learning that is actively pursued for its own sake.

McMenniman distinguishes between four kinds of motivation – task-derived motivation, where it is the simple enjoyment of the task which makes the individual wish to continue their involvement in it; egoistic motivation in which the source is competition with others; social solidarity, where the source is the desire to please others; and fourth, as a means to an end, extrinsic motivation. She argues that it is only really the first of these – enjoyment of the task – which leads to intrinsic motivation and that while extrinsic rewards in the shape of perceived carrots may be acceptable for routine tasks, such rewards also undermine the potential for students to develop intrinsic responsibility as they learn to 'trade for grades'.

By contrast the development of intrinsic motivation is more likely to result in increased conceptual thinking and creativity (1989: 224). McMeniman also stresses the need to provide students with a measure of autonomy and responsibility if intrinsic motivation is to be enhanced.

Self-Esteem and Self-Efficacy

As we have seen, self-esteem also plays a key part in influencing students' orientation to the learning situation. Although some students are motivated by the spur of competition and the glitter of potential reward, many more learn not to try for fear of failing. Students faced with the repeated experience of negative feedback and/or low marks may well develop what Carol Dweck (1989) has called 'learned helplessness' or 'helpless prone' where they typically reduce their effort in order to protect self-esteem through the knowledge they haven't tried very much. Indeed, research by Bandura (1977) revealed that the amount of persistence exhibited by students is a function of how successful they expect to be. Students who have an image of themselves as successful learners are likely to be more motivated than those who have formed a more negative view of themselves.

Dweck further suggests that learners need to be changed from the belief that their IQ is fixed to one in which they believe they can get smarter by trying. As I suggested above, where a student's approach is characterized by 'learnability' this is likely to mean that their 'locus of control' – how much they feel in control of their learning and responsible for it – is internal. They are likely to think that they have the capacity to improve and that the cause for any lack of success lies within themselves and therefore can be addressed. Those with a more 'external' locus of control are, by contrast, more likely to blame other factors – the quality of teaching, interference from other students, the difficulty of the task – and, hence, be more prone to 'stuckness' and dependent on others for support.

The large and complex psychological literature on 'attribution theory' in fact has quite a simple message when it comes to assessment. This is that students from an early age need to be encouraged and trained in taking responsibility for their own learning and to have their confidence built up that with the appropriate investment of time and effort, they can be successful.

Yet contemporary studies of students' perspectives in a range of countries suggest that this is far from the reality experienced by most students. Rather their educational experience is characterized by a sense of powerlessness, with boredom and anxiety replacing each other in a regular succession (Csikszentmihalyi et al. 1993).

One way or another, it is assessment that is the purveyor of such messages. For students the daily diet of evaluative language, which is a pervasive, and probably essential, part of teaching and learning, is regularly reinforced by more formal evaluative communications in the form of marks and grades, a process that ultimately culminates in the 'summing

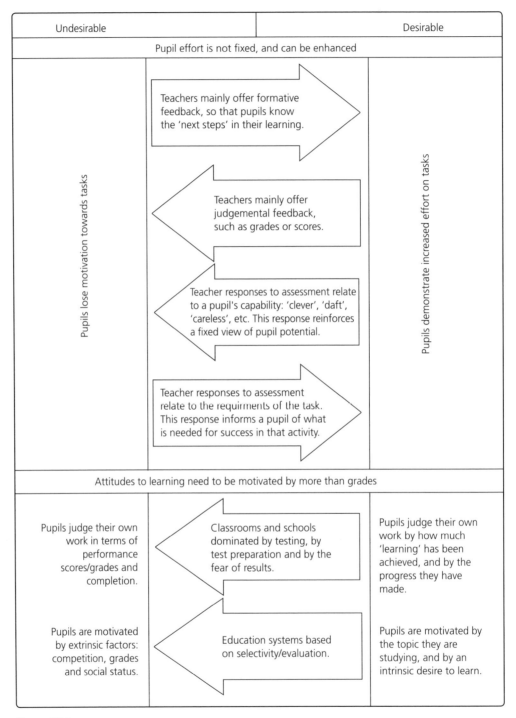

Figure 10.3

up' (Harlen 1994) of the formal examination. Given that in this latter respect, at least, failure is built into the system in that a given proportion of candidates is expected (and often required) to fail, far from growing in confidence, many students label themselves failures very early in their school careers with important consequences for their subsequent capacity and desire to learn.

Yet 'As is our confidence, so is our capacity', wrote the nineteenth-century essayist William Hazlitt. Confidence actually improves the ability to perform, as every athlete knows. Yet many individuals lack confidence in relation to learning. Their progress through school results, for many, in a tendency to fear assessment, to develop strategies for avoiding the teacher's scrutiny, as they fail to achieve success and its coveted accolades.

Activity 10.3

Summative assessment is an integral part of virtually all stages of formal education. How far do you agree with this analysis of its negative effects? Do you agree that, as suggested here, these effects are worse for some students than others? What, if anything, could be done to address these issues?

Self-Regulation and Strategic Awareness

Another of the key learning orientations that is likely to profoundly affect an individual's level of engagement and success is their capacity to be aware of and manage their own learning. This involves being aware of their personal pattern of strengths and weaknesses and using this knowledge, together with a clear understanding of the learning goals being pursued, to work in the way that is most effective for them personally to achieve them. Such a view of learning is in stark contrast to the more conventional 'empty vessel' perspective, which starts from the typically unexamined view of education that a teacher's job is simply to impart knowledge to 'fill up' the student's mind. It is this view of what it is to learn that is so often associated with forms of testing and assessment that are merely focused on the lowest-order cognitive skill of recall. Yet,

> The view of learning that underlies standardized test theory is inconsistent with the view rapidly emerging from cognitive and educational psychology. Learners become more competent not simply by learning more facts and skills, but by reconfiguring their knowledge, by chunking information to reduce memory loads and by designing strategies and models that help them discern when and how facts and skills are important. (Mislevy et al. 1991: 1)

Many experiments have been done to explore how much difference training in such 'metacognitive' skills can make. Merrett and Merrett (1992), for example, describe a study in which an experimental group were asked to monitor their level of engagement and whether they were on task or not every time a bell rung. They found that even this simple device resulted in a significant improvement in the learning of the experimental group over the control group because it helped to train the students' metacognitve awareness. Many other studies have had similarly significant results (Quicke and Winter 1994).

It is clear, then, that one of the most constructive ways of spending classroom time is that invested in training students to be better at managing themselves as learners. Herein lies the rationale for much of the contemporary development of portfolio and personal development planning schemes such as the current requirement in England for all students in higher education to be provided with access to a 'Progress File' in which they can record past achievements, reflect on progress and plan future learning goals (Jackson 2001). We shall discuss these schemes in more detail in the next chapter.

However, providing students with the opportunity to develop the capacity to be self-managing learners also implies giving them a measure of autonomy in the learning process. While this may be an accepted feature of many higher education courses, it is not typical of the traditional, teacher-dominated school classroom. Moreover, as the volume and significance of summative testing is increasing, students find themselves with correspondingly less autonomy as the requirement to ensure adequate coverage of the exam syllabus drives out apparently less important priorities.

Support and Feedback

Finally, in this exploration of the key factors that affect learning, we turn to a brief consideration of the social context of learning. Although it is typically regarded as an individual pursuit and achievement, learning is in fact an essentially social activity. It typically requires some kind of intervention to provide help and guidance – 'the teaching role' – though this can come in many forms and some kind of feedback regarding progress. Moreover, people learn through sharing ideas, through collaboration and teamwork, through talking about things.

Recognition of the key role that social interaction plays in learning owes a great deal to the work of Vygotsky and his concept of the 'zone of proximal development' which he defined as: 'the distance between the actual developmental level as determined through independent problem solving and the level of potential development as determined through problem solving under adult guidance or in collaboration with more capable peers' (Vygotsky 1978: 86). The ZPD, he suggested, has four stages. The first stage is where performance is assisted by more capable others, such as parents, teachers or peers. The second is where the learner's performance becomes self-assisted. The third is where performance has developed to such a stage that it has become internalized and almost automatic; and the fourth is where the learner becomes aware of new areas to learn and has to cope with the knowledge of this uncertainty.

Herein lies the importance of formative assessment. 'Teaching can be said to occur when assistance is offered at points in the ZPD at which performance requires assistance. Careful assessment of the child's abilities relative to the ZPD and the developmental level is a constant requirement for the teacher' (Tharpe and Gallimore 1988: 41–2). Such assistance may take a number of forms, for example, modelling the desired learning as behaviour for imitation; offering rewards and punishment to encourage appropriate developments; feedback on performance; questioning to discover the level of a student's ability or understanding; and, last but not least, instructing – the most ubiquitous means of assisting learning in ordinary life. But whatever the form of intervention a teacher chooses, its effectiveness depends on the teacher's sensitive and accurate assessment of a learner's needs.

But while both children and adults must confront areas of relative uncertainty and ignorance, children are in a particularly challenging position as learners because their intellectual areas of uncertainty are systematically confronted by the school curriculum, while adults are able to manage their lives in order to avoid unwelcome challenges to new learning. Moreover, students within educational institutions learn in an explicitly evaluative environment which means that their confidence, their self-esteem and their relationships with peers are constantly subject to potential attack.

As we have seen, effective learning depends on students having a clear understanding of their individual strengths and weaknesses, styles and preferences as learners plus a clear understanding of their learning goals and what will constitute success. This means that students need the opportunity both to receive feedback and to engage in some form of reflective dialogue.

The following quotations provide powerful testimony to these arguments. The first group are from two young children in primary schools and the second, from university students, demonstrating that the importance of good formative assessment holds true whatever the age and level of the learner. Sadly these quotations also illustrate the much more common reality of learners who are unclear about what would constitute good performance, and are hence entirely dependent on the teacher to guide them as to how far their work is good with the associated anxiety involved in this.

In answer to the question 'How do you feel when your teacher asks to look at your work?', these young children replied:

> Yes, if I think I haven't done much or if I have rushed because I didn't feel like it, I feel a bit worried, but if I think it looks nice I am proud for her to see it.

> I am worried – I go like this (mimes praying). You never know when she does a line if it's going to go like this or like this (mimes cross and tick). When she marks them right I am so happy. A bit disappointed if wrong.

Yes, but not when I am in the middle of something 'cos I like to get on with it. I feel that I have finished it at last. Sometimes I have to say I don't like work or the others in my class call me a wimp. (Pollard et al. 2000)

Learning interactions clearly do not just relate to the task itself. They are also a vital element in shaping the effective context for learning, providing encouragement and helping to build the learner's confidence and sense of self, as discussed above. As an evaluative dialogue, assessment is clearly central to the social context of learning but particularly as the mechanism for providing feedback to guide future efforts and encouragement to sustain motivation. Consequently, the issue of how to provide effective feedback now looms large in discussions of formative assessment.

Thus in the world of education, we now find ourselves in a situation in which we know a great deal from research about what kind of assessment will be most effective in developing student 'learning power'. This is assessment that facilitates student engagement in, and ownership of, the task in hand, motivation, confidence, self-esteem and supportive personal relationships. We also know that the impact of the high-stakes, summative assessment that is currently so popular is very different. For example, a recent review of the research evidence concerning the impact of summative assessment on students' learning by Harlen and Deakin-Crick (2002) identified the following key findings:

Argument against formative ass

- Summative assessment encourages teachers to adopt transmission teaching.
- 'High-stakes' tests drive classroom activity and priorities.
- Practising tests reinforces low self-esteem among lower-achievers.
- 'High-stakes' tests lower the self-esteem of lower-achieving students.
- Students react to a 'performance' ethos.
- Students become increasingly anxious.
- Students' effort is affected by their perceived sense of achievement.
- Students adjust their future effort in response to feedback.
- Students become increasingly extrinsically motivated and grade obsessed.
- Girls and lower-achievers are worst affected.

A similar picture emerges from research in the United States (Madaus and Clarke 1991) where policy agendas are increasingly characterized by a reliance on high-stakes tests to raise standards. The research challenges the fundamental rationale for the growing test culture in finding that high-stakes tests:

- do not have a markedly positive effect on teaching and learning in the classroom;
- do not motivate the unmotivated;
- contrary to popular belief, 'authentic' forms of high-stakes assessment are not a more equitable way to assess the progress of students who differ in race, culture, native language or gender;
- increase high school dropout rates – particularly among minority student populations.

So, not only are more traditional forms of summative assessment, especially tests and examinations, liable to considerable weaknesses in their own terms regarding reliability and validity, they also appear to exert a significantly damaging effect on the day-to-day business of learning.

Perhaps most surprising, in the light of these findings, is the lack of attention that is typically given to what both evidence and experience suggest is the huge emotional impact of assessment on students (Broadfoot 2003). As we have seen in previous chapters, there are good reasons for the persistence of this apparently anomalous situation. However it can, and should, be addressed if the huge resources being invested in education are truly to produce value for money in that the students of today will emerge as the lifelong learning citizens and workers of tomorrow. We now know a great deal about how assessment *can* be used to support learning and in the final part of this chapter on 'the emerging evidence' it is to a brief discussion of these important new insights that we now turn.

Using Feedback to Support Learning

As we have seen, closely related to the issue of students' feelings about their learning, is their capacity to be empowered and self-directing learners. The research evidence available suggests that the greatest motivational benefits will come from feedback that focuses on the quality of the students' work rather than on comparisons with other students; on specific ways in which the students' work can be improved and on improvements that the students have made compared to their earlier work (Crooks 2001). For 'students have to be active in their own learning (teachers cannot learn for them) and unless they come to understand their own strengths and weaknesses and how they might deal with them they will not make progress' (Harlen and James 1997).

For this to be possible, students need a clear understanding of the assessment criteria that will be applied to judging the success of their work (Torrance and Coultas 2004). Feedback is well-defined as: 'the communication of information about the standard of the performance; or as an active force which fills the gap between actual and desired performance. Feedback which involves change involves students' understanding the concepts of quality held by those making judgements' (Sadler 1989).

Students also need feedback that is encouraging and builds their confidence, that has a positive *emotional* as well as *intellectual* impact. To quote Sadler:

> By quality of feedback we now realize we have to understand not just the technical structure of the feedback (such as accuracy, comprehensiveness and appropriateness) but also its accessibility to the learner (as a communication) its catalytic and coaching value and its ability to inspire confidence and hope. (Sadler 1989)

This point is well-demonstrated by the results of a simple experiment reported by Paul Black – a longstanding protagonist for good formative assessment:

> Three matched groups of students were subject to different assessment approaches. The first group received only marks; the second, marks and grades; the third, comments only. All three groups undertook a pre-test and a post-test to compare their relative progress. It was found that the first two groups made no gains whereas the third achieved a 30% gain.
>
> A more subtle version of this experiment involved various combinations of types of feedback: group 1 received comments, group 2 received grades; group 3 received praise and group 4, no feedback at all. Group 1's progress proved to be more than that of the other three groups combined. It was further found that the use of grades and praise encouraged extrinsic motivation and hence, not the most productive form of involvement in learning. This is because feedback given as rewards or grades enhances ego rather than task involvement and can damage the self-esteem of low attainers. By contrast, in a task-oriented system all attribution of success is to effort and learning is improved particularly amongst low attainers. (Black 2003)

It is essential that students understand what they need to do to improve. Feedback must be sufficiently clear that it enables learners to 'close the gap' between their current position and their desired achievement. But it is also desirable that the feedback provided enhances a student's more general 'learning power' in terms of their motivation, confidence and strategic awareness of their own learning strengths and weaknesses. It follows that students must be trained in the capacity to monitor their own work and be motivated so to do.

However, many classroom assessments are hard to articulate in terms of explicit criteria because they are based on so-called 'fuzzy criteria'. Research reveals that many students in primary and secondary schools do not understand the feedback they get from teachers as a result of marking and grading and that it frequently offers little guidance about how to improve. Indeed a good deal of the time, such marks and grades appear to be almost random as far as students were concerned, occasioning often anger and frustration as well as occasional delighted surprise. Not surprisingly, the effect of assessment on learners is often very different from that which the teacher intends (Weeden et al. 2002).

Activity 10.4

Consider your own experience of receiving feedback on your work. In what form was it most useful and why?

Sadler, who, as we have seen, is a leading exponent of the importance of feedback, refers to this as teachers' 'guild knowledge' – the intuitive understanding of the appropriate standard which is possessed by teachers as a result of their professional training and experience. Sadler stresses the need for teachers to translate these holistic, qualitative judgements, their intuitive understanding of the learning goals being pursued into terms that will be meaningful to students. This can be done, he argues, through training students to develop their capacity to generate equivalent 'guild knowledge' about desired standards through a triangulation of descriptive statements, practice and the use of exemplar material.

> The indispensable conditions for improvement are that the student comes to hold a concept of quality roughly similar to that being held by the teacher, is able to monitor continuously the quality of what is being produced during the act of production itself and has a repertoire of alternative moves or strategies from which to draw at any given point. In other words, students have to be able to judge the quality of what they are producing and be able to regulate what they are doing during the doing of it. (Sadler 1989)

These points are summarized in the figure below which comes from a training manual for teachers (M. Clarke, 'How Am I Doing?', p. 3).

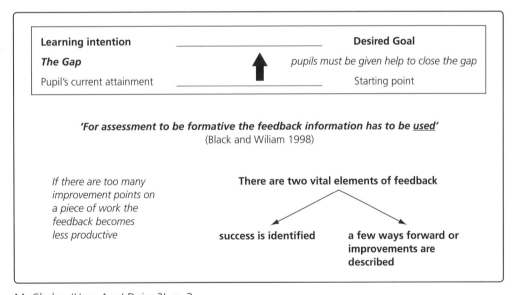

M. Clarke, 'How Am I Doing?', p. 3

Dann (2002) proposes that 'meta-learning' (Watkins et al. 2001), or 'learning to learn', is an essential aspect of self-assessment and learning. She argues that 'a focus on the processes of learning, rather than the required outcome that is, performance, is most likely actually to improve learning and subsequently performance too' (p. 111).

The clear and powerful conclusions of research in the area of assessment and learning are cogently summarized by Black and William (1998) in an influential article that updates the earlier work of Crooks on assessment and classroom learning. The research confirms that improving learning through assessment depends on the following factors:

- A recognition of the profound influence assessment has on the motivation and self-esteem of pupils both of which are crucial influences on learning.
- The creation of a classroom culture based on mutual respect.
- The active involvement of pupils in their own learning and in self-assessment.
- The provision of effective feedback to pupils which allows them to recognize the next steps and how to take them.
- A view of teaching and learning in which feedback is seen as an essential part.
- Adjusting teaching to take account of the results of assessment.
- Sharing learning goals with pupils.
- The need for pupils to be able to assess themselves and understand how to improve.
- Helping students to know and to recognize the standards they are aiming for.
- The confidence that every student can improve.
- Both teacher and pupils reviewing and reflecting on assessment data.

There is now considerable research evidence to support these conclusions (Black et al. 2003; Earl 2003). Moreover, the evidence suggests that, if applied, the impact on learning outcomes would be considerable. In their comprehensive review, for example, Black and Wiliam provide the following summary of the scale of the potential effects:

> in short a range of current studies involving 5 year olds to university students across a range of subjects and international settings show that innovations which include strengthening the practice of formative assessment all produce significant and often substantial learning gains. Effect sizes are typically between 0.4 and 0.7 where 'effect size' is defined as the measure of the learning advantage over a control group as a fraction of a measure of the spread of attainment among the students. For example an effect size of 0.7 would have raised England's score in the third international maths and science study from the middle of 41 countries to being in the top 5. Moreover, improved formative assessment helps low attainers more than the rest. (Black and Wiliam 1998)

Thus, assessment will enhance learning if it can be designed to:

- encourage intrinsic motivation;
- build learner confidence;
- give learners a sense of ownership and control;
- provide detailed feedback;
- enhance learners' strategic awareness;
- encourage collaboration between students.

The work of many scholars in the field of learning and assessment has recently been summarized for the benefit of policy-makers and practitioners by the Assessment Reform Group in their Ten Principles of Assessment for Learning.

Ten Principles of Assessment for Learning

The principles are substantiated in each case by significant bodies of research, as well as by the evidence of development studies which have recently been initiated. Thus, there is now a clear blueprint for moving forward on the assessment for learning agenda which seems likely to gather momentum rapidly in an international climate, for too long dominated by an obsession with ranking and comparing, and the powerful forces of the status quo.

1 is part of effective planning;
2 focuses on how students learn;
3 is central to classroom practice;
4 is a key professional skill;
5 is sensitive and constructive;
6 fosters motivation;
7 promotes understanding of goals and criteria;
8 helps learners know how to improve;
9 develops the capacity for self-assessment;
10 recognizes all educational achievement. (Assessment Reform Group 2002)

To the extent that these findings are valid, they highlight a powerful cocktail of influences at work in any learning setting. As such, it is remarkable that they have, until recently, received so little professional attention; that thinking about assessment has been largely confined to improving the capacity to *describe* students' achievements. Indeed, it would appear that the reality of daily classroom life is very different from that described above. There is, rather,

- a tendency for teachers to assess quantity of work and presentation rather than the quality of learning;
- greater attention given to marking and grading, much of it tending to lower the self-esteem of pupils rather than providing advice for improvement;
- a strong emphasis on comparing pupils with each other, which demoralizes the less successful learners;
- teachers' feedback to pupils often serving social and managerial purposes rather than helping them to learn more effectively;
- teachers not knowing enough about their pupils' learning needs;
- teachers' tests tending to encourage rote and superficial learning;
- insufficient discussion between teachers in schools as to whether they are really assessing what is important.

The same problems are characteristic of further and higher education as well as schools. The quotations below are from students in higher education collected as part of the self-assessment in professional higher education (SAPHE Project):

> If your work is OK or if you get a really high mark then you just get a 'tick' or 'excellent' and I find that totally infuriating. You've got an idea what was good but you don't know where the other 20% went or how you could have picked up more marks. I'm not looking for perfection but I need to know what it would have taken me to get the extra percentage, what they were looking for.

> I'd like the feedback to be a bit more personal but there are lots of students and I suppose the lecturers can't spend all their time giving feedback.

> I'd love the opportunity to sit down with the person who has marked my work and go through it with them but it's not going to happen.

> I try and read the comments and make note of them for next time but I don't feel involved. I feel like a number.

> On a daily basis you don't feel part of a two-way process at all because you don't have contact with the people you are supposed to be learning from. I've adopted the attitude now that if I want this degree I'm going to have to get on with it. Whether I do it with the aid of a lecturer doesn't matter to me.

> It should be to judge what we have learned and how good the teaching is but I think it is just a way of categorizing us all.

Clearly, a great deal needs to be done at national policy level as well as in the initial and in-service training to help teachers develop these better feedback skills and a greater commitment to its importance for learners.

Summary

This chapter has had a profound but simple message. Assessment exercises a profound effect on students' day-to-day engagement with the learning process. There can be little doubt that whatever the approach to assessment that is used, and whatever its purpose, it influences student learning profoundly. Indeed it is perhaps *the* defining element in classroom life. This is because it

- helps to identify the appropriate starting point for instruction;
- makes learning goals clear;
- influences students' learning strategies and skills;
- influences students' ability to attain and apply learning;
- influences students' self-perceptions concerning self-efficacy;
- influences students' motivation.

In short, assessment

> guides their judgement as to what is important to learn, affects their motivation and self-
> perceptions of competence, structures their approaches in timing of personal study, consoli-
> dates learning and affects the development of enduring learning strategies and skills. It appears
> to be one of the most urgent forces influencing education. Accordingly, it deserves very careful
> planning and considerable investment in time from educators. (Crooks 1998)

Assessment is also arguably one of the defining elements of life beyond formal educational settings. As opportunities to learn grow exponentially through the availability of a myriad of online resources, so it becomes daily more important that everyone can take advantage of these. This is not only vital for the economy and for individuals seeking jobs within it; it is also important for the simple reason that people derive great pleasure and satisfaction from learning, and that their learning in turn enriches society. Assessment that supports learners both in formal education and beyond, must be '*sustainable*' in that it 'encompasses the abilities required to undertake those activities that necessarily accompany learning throughout life in formal and in informal settings' (Boud 2002).

The components of such sustainable assessment are the key elements of assessment for learning, which has been the subject of this chapter. These are:

- a belief that all students can succeed is needed;
- a recognition that learners' beliefs about their own capacity as learners can affect achievement;
- the separation of feedback from grading;
- the focus of assessment on learning rather than on performance;
- the development of self-assessment as central;
- recognition that reflective assessment with peers is valuable;
- that for assessment to be formative, it has to be used.

Yet despite this now longstanding evidence concerning the very significant role played by assessment in the learning process, such understanding has yet to challenge the prevailing international policy discourse. What was described in Chapter 7 as 'the quality agenda' still predominates with its emphasis on monitoring and accountability leading to increasingly 'high-stakes' external tests with their necessary premium on reliability. Where teachers feel under pressure to 'teach the test', so the opportunities for exploring the potential of 'assessment for learning', are correspondingly diminished (Pollard et al. 1994; Pollard et al. 2000). The development of 'assessment literacy' more generally as part of teachers' professional skills also becomes less of a priority.

It is clear that as educators, we are missing a lot of tricks. We are doing things which we ought not to do and we are failing to do the things we ought to do. There is powerful evidence to suggest that our current assessment practices are damaging to the learning careers of many students. At the same time, there is clear guidance available concerning how we could remedy this situation in readily practicable ways. There is little evidence that piling on the pressure in terms of ever more tests and exams is raising standards as a whole (although it may for a time raise test results), and a good deal to suggest that this is having a negative effect on the confidence and motivation of many students.

By contrast, using assessment to *support* learning, rather than simply to *judge* it, may be the most powerful tool we have to improve educational outcomes. Certainly, recent experience with attempts to improve formative assessment practices is encouraging and this is the focus of the next chapter for, in the words of the Assessment Reform Group: 'Assessment which is explicitly designed to promote learning is the single most powerful tool we have for raising standards and empowering lifelong learners' (ARG 1999).

Key references

Black, P. and Wiliam, D. (1998) 'Assessment and Classroom Learning'. *Assessment in Education* Volume 5, Number 1, pp. 7–74.

Crooks, T. (1988) 'The Impact of Classroom Evaluation Practices on Students'. *Review of Educational Research* Volume 58, Number 4 (Winter), pp. 438–81.

Harlen, W. and James, M. (1997) 'Assessment and Learning: Differences and relationships between formative and summative assessment'. *Assessment in Education* Volume 4, Number 3, pp. 365–79.

Useful websites

http://assessment-reform-group.org/
The aim of the Assessment Reform Group (ARG) is to ensure that assessment policy and practice at all levels takes account of relevant research evidence. In pursuit of this aim the main targets for the group's activity are policy-makers in government and its agencies. It also works closely with teachers, teacher organizations and Local Education Authority staff to advance understanding of the roles, purposes and impacts of assessment.

http://www.tlrp.org/
The website of The Economic and Social Research Council (ESRC)'s Teaching and Learning Research Programme giving access to information and links to 60+ projects across the four countries of the UK, many of which provide research evidence concerning the assessment themes discussed in this chapter.

New Vision, New Tools: Feedback, Self-Assessment and Portfolios

Legislation alone will not improve the quality of learning in the classroom, nor will it raise the attainment of young people. Only when they fully understand what is happening to them, and are actively involved in the educational process, will all this actually happen. (Ruth Sutton 2000)

In the last chapter, we explored the arguments for thinking about assessment in a radically new way, namely, its role in promoting learning. We explored the crucial importance of taking into account the feelings that assessment engenders, and the need to understand 'what works' in helping students to learn better. It is clear from research evidence that learning increases if:

- teachers communicate clear and high expectations to students;
- teachers avoid using marks and grades;
- timely and detailed feedback is provided that focuses on the task rather than the student;
- teachers offer guidance about next steps;
- teachers clarify what success looks like.

This is partly because students are thus enabled to work 'smarter', but equally because such approaches empower students as partners in the learning process and, as such, have a powerful effect on motivation, which is the engine of learning.

Practising formative assessment necessarily involves learners in taking a share of the responsibility for the organization of their work, keeping their own records of activities they have undertaken and achievements and making their own decisions about future actions and targets. A moment's thought will reveal that provision for such active and democratic student engagement in the learning process may be difficult for teachers trained in a more classical transmission mode of teaching to accept, and also difficult to implement unless there is a reprioritization of classroom activities.

Yet, it would be hard to quarrel with this assertion, made about higher education explicitly, but clearly more generally relevant that:

> In an era in which the espoused values of Higher Education are independence of thought, personal development and the ability to reflect on one's own practice and to use feedback to assess and manage one's performance through self-reflection, the paradigms of assessment which concentrate on the acquisition of content knowledge are outdated. (Atkins 1995)

Indeed many recent studies show that, not only is this possible to achieve where teachers are given support and encouragement to develop their practice, but that it is also very rewarding for teachers when they do make such a shift of emphasis (Natriello 1987; Black et al. 2003).

A mass of international evidence assembled by the OECD, and others, documents the powerful impact that formative assessment is now having in many different countries (CERI 2005). In pursuing better formative assessment, teachers have shifted their role from one of presentation to one of exploring student ideas, including expending time and effort to frame questions to permit such exploration. As students have become more active participants in the learning process, they have come to realize that learning may depend less on their capacity to spot right answers and more on their readiness to express and discuss their own understanding. Teachers have been challenged to compose useful comments that students can and want to read. Teachers have changed their view of the role of written work in promoting student learning and have had to give more attention to differentiation in the feedback they provide. Students, in their turn, take note of teachers' comments and use these to improve their work as well as changing their perception of the role of written work in learning.

In short, it is clear that teachers need to:

- start from a learner's existing understanding in order to involve the learner actively in the learning process;
- encourage students to develop a sense of themselves as learners which includes a view of their own purpose for learning;
- teach students how to assess their progress as they proceed, keeping the aims and criteria of a particular learning task in mind – so that they can become more independent learners;

- ensure that students are clear what constitutes quality work in that students understand the assessment criteria being used so they can apply them themselves (in many cases, where these criteria are abstract, modelling exercises are likely to be needed);
- teach students to collaborate in peer assessment since this helps them to develop their capacity for objectivity as well as their understanding of the assessment criteria. The social dimension of classroom interaction involving constructive, focused discussion between students themselves and with the teacher is crucial in developing a supportive culture for learning. (Black et al. 2003)

A significant finding is that the adoption of this kind of formative assessment can significantly increase performance in conventional school assessments and traditional public examinations. A recent study in the UK, for example, found that the use of formative assessment produced an effect size of 0.32 even in the context of continuing high-stakes assessment (Wiliam et al. 2004). Therefore, 'At the very least these data suggest that teachers do not have to choose between teaching well and getting good results' (Wiliam and Blee 2001).

This very significant finding contradicts the earlier, much less optimistic observation by the leading Swiss psychologist, Phillipe Perrenoud:

> there are few who will resolutely and openly oppose differentiated education or formative assessment provided that these are 'extras' and do not compromise any of the traditional functions of assessment or the school system, disrupt parents' habits or require teachers to obtain new skills! (Perrenoud 1989)

As with other educational innovations success in this respect appears to be associated with careful, professional management including:

- building on existing practice aiming to complement it rather than to replace it;
- providing staff training and opportunities for staff to practise reflective exercises;
- providing an induction and rationale for students;
- sharing practice with others;
- being realistic about what is possible, accepting small changes rather than attempting wholesale revolution;
- integration at appropriate and relevant points.

As with any such innovation, its success is likely to be highly dependent on explicit senior management commitment and institutional leadership, on careful planning and the provision of necessary resources. It will involve the sustained management of change involving mutual support between colleagues and effective communication with students and their parents. Last but not least, the positive potential of student self-assessment is likely to be greatly influenced by the national policy context and practitioners' perspectives of 'what counts'. As we have seen, the prevailing policy context is not felicitous to such initiatives at present. Their rapid growth despite this is testimony to the positive experience of teachers who have sought to implement such approaches and the growing evidence that they can enhance students' performance significantly.

In what follows, we examine some of the ways in which this kind of learning partnership can be realized in practice. We begin with the notion of student self-assessment, since this is one of the most central ideas of assessment for learning.

Activity 11.1

Consider any educational innovation that you have been involved in. How successful was it? What were the main barriers to change that you needed to overcome?

Student Self-Assessment

It is clear that the powerful potential of good formative assessment will depend to a great extent on the enthusiasm and commitment of teachers, and indeed students, who are often some of the most conservative forces in the educational process. Enhancing educators' professional skills with regard to formative assessment will clearly be vital in this regard. However, there are good grounds now for thinking that this is likely to be possible and, indeed, enthusiastically received by teachers since it is now apparent that such improved professional skills can be readily developed in normal classroom settings.

There are many examples that could be cited of the practical realization of the ideas underpinning assessment and learning. These can be found at every level of the education system, from nurseries to higher professional qualifications. No learner is too young to be able to take responsibility for their own learning, and none is so successful that they cannot benefit from honing their self-reflection skills. There are many examples of strategies that have been successfully used in primary-school classrooms to enable children to take ownership of their learning through better use of feedback, self-assessment and more reflective practice (Clarke 2001).

In higher education too, where novel assessment practices are perhaps least well-developed, significant strides have also been made in instituting self-assessment. One of the most thorough studies was designed to explore how self-assessment could best be introduced in the context of professional higher education – in this case, Law and Social Work. This project found that:

- Such novel assessment practices were most likely to take root when they built on existing practice, aiming to complement, rather than to replace, it.

- There was a substantial need for staff training and for opportunities for staff themselves to practise the kind of reflective exercises they were requesting students to undertake.
- There needed to be provision for induction and explanation for students, most of whom are unfamiliar with this kind of thinking and practice and hence are often initially hostile to it.
- Teachers, subject departments and even whole institutions could benefit a great deal by sharing insights and experiences with each other. (Hinett and Thomas 1999)

During recent decades the notion of student involvement in the assessment process, particularly in the form of student self-assessment, has grown rapidly in acceptability. Whereas an early study undertaken by the author (Broadfoot 1979) revealed an almost complete lack of research literature on this subject, recent years have produced a very considerable body of both theoretical and applied research aimed at exploring both the rationale for, and the effective use of, student self-assessment. Thus there is now a considerable platform on which to build.

Briefly, self-assessment is a review process which involves the student in:

- reflecting upon past experience;
- evaluating it and attempting to articulate what has been learned; and
- identifying in the light of this reflection, what still needs to be pursued.

It has significant implications for the organization of teaching and learning in that it cedes some measure of control over one of the teacher's most powerful tools, namely assessment, to the learners themselves.

Boud (1991) defines self-assessment as follows:

> Self-assessment requires students to think critically about what they are learning, to identify appropriate standards of performance and to apply them to their own work. Self-assessment encourages students to look to themselves and to other sources to determine what criteria should be used in judging their work rather than being dependent solely on their teachers or other authorities ...

Self-assessment, therefore, is not really just an assessment practice; it is actually a learning activity. It is a way of encouraging students to reflect on what they have learned so far, to think about ways of improving their learning and to make plans which will enable them to progress as learners and to reach their goals. Self-assessment encourages students to reflect on their work, to be critical about their strengths and weaknesses and crucially to take responsibility for their own progress. As such it incorporates the skills of time-management, action-planning, negotiation, interpersonal skills, communication – with both teachers and fellow students – and self-discipline in addition to reflection, critical judgement and evaluation.

Students involved in self-assessment are more likely to wish to continue their learning and to know how to do so; to monitor their own performance without constant reference to the teacher; and to take full responsibility for their actions and judgements. In short, in being encouraged to engage in self-assessment they are being trained with the '3 Rs' which are likely to be crucial for learning success in the twenty-first century, namely, Resourcefulness, Reflection and Resilience.

Yet, 'whilst it has been well documented that self-assessment is beneficial to both the children and the teachers, not a lot has been done that takes self-assessment beyond reflection on what was learnt and what was liked to a higher level of intellectual quality and student engagement ... self-assessment is not only a vehicle for accessing children's learning and ensuring substantive engagement occurs but it is also a way of thinking, a philosophy of teaching and learning' (Munns and Woodward 2004: 2).

If the use of self-assessment is truly to deliver its potential benefits, it must be part of an approach to teaching and learning that recognizes the central role of student engagement and its association with their need to become 'insiders' in the learning culture of their classrooms, 'insiders' whose intellect and emotions are fully brought to bear on the task in hand. Table 11.1 below illustrates the different dimensions and levels of self-assessment and, as such, emphasizes the need for both students and teachers to be trained in the relevant understanding and skills.

The notion of self-assessment is quite a challenging one and it would be wrong not to articulate the difficulties that can be encountered in seeking to introduce it. First, it differs from its first cousin – reflection – in being more explicitly concerned with the making of judgements about aspects of achievement – sometimes in ways that must be publicly defensible. Where self-assessment is part of the formal assessment for a particular unit of learning, for example, there may be issues to do with agreeing the criteria to be used and how far the student's assessment is likely to concur with, say, that of the teacher. Although research has shown that there is no overall consistent tendency either to over- or underestimate performance when students assess themselves, the potential for student and teacher to agree grades is likely to be enhanced where they have collaborated in the process of generating assessment criteria (Falchikov and Boud 1989).

If, however, the self-assessment is not intended to contribute directly to an explicit judgement of performance, there can be difficulties in encouraging students to take the process seriously. At best, the process is likely still to be an unfamiliar one. At worst, it will be resisted by students as an unreasonable imposition in addition to the learning process itself.

The rationale for a particular self-assessment – whether it is intended to enhance learning or simply to share the assessment load, for example – is likely to affect students' attitudes to it. All the various vehicles for self-assessment such as learning logs, portfolios and reflective diaries, as well as more one-off opportunities to comment on particular pieces of work, raise the same questions about fitness for purpose that were identified in Chapter 1. Once again,

Table 11.1 What Counts as Good Self-Assessment?

When	But not when
the motive for its introduction is related to enhancing learning	it is related to meeting institutional or other external requirements
it is designed specifically with both subject-matter and learning outcomes in mind	a self-assessment strategy is borrowed from another context without detailed adaptation
it is introduced with a clear rationale	it is treated as another course requirement
it is treated as a central aspect of learning	it is used simply as an assessment device
it has a significant educational role to play regardless of whether workloads change	it is used primarily to reduce staff workloads
students' concerns are fully addressed	there are no opportunities to question it and adapt in the light of student needs
learners are involved in establishing criteria	learners are using criteria determined solely by others
learners have a direct role in influencing the process	the process is imposed on them
it makes an identifiable contribution to formal decision-making	no use is formally made of the outcomes
it is one of a number of complementary strategies to promote self-directed and interdependent learning	it is tacked on to an existing subject in isolation from other strategies
its practices permeate the total course	it is marginalized as part of subjects which have low status
staff are willing to share control of assessment and do so	staff retain all control (sometimes despite appearances otherwise)
qualitative peer feedback is used as part of the process	it is subordinated to quantitative peer assessment
it is part of a profiling process in which students have an active role	records about students are produced with no input from them
activities are introduced in step with students' capabilities in learning-how-to-learn	it is a one-off event

of critical importance is the need for the assessment to be designed with a clear purpose in mind. If, for example, the learning log is intended to be a private vehicle for a student to reflect on as part of their own learning, it would not then be appropriate for it to be used as a component in the overall assessment of a course. If, on the other hand, as is the case with many types of professional training, a reflective learning portfolio is an integral part of the assessment of professional competence, then the design of the self-assessment contained therein is likely to be very different.

It is clear that self-assessment in itself is not a panacea; in itself it is simply a different answer to the question of who is assessing. The other questions of 'why', 'how' and so on, identified in Chapter 1, are just as relevant for self-assessment as they are for assessment carried out by others, such as teachers or examiners. However, the importance of a clear link between purpose and procedure is arguably even more important in the case of self-assessment because the students are necessarily exposing more of themselves to assessment scrutiny.

Indeed, there is a very real danger that self-assessment could become as much a pressure for conformity and, hence, a source of social control, rather than a means of empowering students in the way intended (Broadfoot 1990, 1998a). This is because it is all too easy to introduce self-assessment in name only, while leaving the fundamentals of classroom activity unchanged. This is likely to be worse than useless in its impact on the quality of student learning.

Tools for the Trade

Portfolios

Many of the recent developments in assessment approaches build on the logic that has been discussed here. Increasingly popular, particularly in many professional learning contexts, is the completion of a reflective portfolio, in which the student builds up a file of self-assessments, including personal reflection and evidence, to form a learning diary (Klenowski 2002). Such 'portfolios' have the double benefit of providing evidence, not only of the outcome of the student's learning, but also of the quality of the learning process itself. There is now a growing body of research evidence that even very young children can use portfolios effectively to support the development of their learning dispositions (Carr and Claxton 2002; Carr 2004).

Moreover, in preparing their portfolio, students are enhancing their ability to reflect critically on their own development. Given that – as we saw in Chapter 10 – the capacity to monitor one's own learning actively – what was referred to there as 'metacognition' – is a central element of becoming an effective learner, portfolio preparation therefore represents a very useful tool in promoting the use of assessment to support learning.

Portfolios also have the further advantage of a very high level of validity in that the evidence they contain can be designed to link very closely to the subject being studied and the desired learning goals. However, they are typically very individual documents – a record of a student's progress on teaching practice, for example, or the basis for an employee's annual appraisal. As such, they do not readily lend themselves to comparison with the achievements of other learners. Indeed, as with any kind of self-assessment, the potential sensitivity of the process of personal reflection is an important issue.

It is, therefore, vital that the purpose and nature of the portfolio exercise are clear to all concerned from the outset. Portfolios can also be successfully used in much more summative ways – such as for an art examination – where it is the quality of the critical commentary in cognitive terms that is the focus of assessment. Once again it is the issue of fitness for purpose that is paramount – choosing and using assessment tools in an informed way so that they are best suited to achieve the goal in question.

Activity 11.2

Think of an example of an assessment portfolio with which you are familiar. How useful do you think it is in a) supporting the process of learning; b) providing summative evidence of achievement?

Records of achievement

Records of achievement are a close relative to portfolios. They represent one of the first attempts by the educational community to address the demotivating effects of conventional summative assessment in which many will not achieve success. Ironically perhaps, it was in an attempt to find an alternative form of *summative* certification for such students, that the educational community began to stumble on far more significant insights concerning how assessment might be used to transform the process of teaching and learning itself. In the UK the Records of Achievement movement started several decades ago with the idea that by broadening the range of achievements that could be formally acknowledged in a school-leaving document, this would improve the motivation of students that could not hope to succeed in public examinations – that such a broadly based record encompassing information about personal experience, achievements and qualities, as well as vocational skills, would improve students' extrinsic motivation.

While experience in practice was to prove this assumption flawed, the teachers committed to the initiative came to realize that something else *was* making an apparent difference in both student motivation and the quality of their learning. This was not the intended new system of *communication* of achievement as a source of extrinsic motivation, but rather derived from assessment as *curriculum*, from the increased intrinsic motivation that was being brought about by changes in the teaching and learning process itself.

Such changes included sharing and discussing curriculum goals with students; encouraging students to set their own learning targets and to draw up more general action plans; involving students in assessing their own work so that they became more able and, hence, more willing, to monitor their own learning; and teachers and students reviewing progress together. It was the opportunity to discuss their progress, their aspirations and their worries on a one-to-one basis with a teacher that for many students made a particular impact, since many of them had never before had the chance of an individual conversation with a teacher about their learning (Broadfoot *et al.* 1984; Broadfoot 1990).

This very simple expedient clearly presented many practical challenges for schools and remains largely unresolved. It underlines how difficult it is to introduce what are, in effect, quite simple innovations in classroom practice while priorities continue to be dictated by the perceived demands of preparation for traditional examinations. The Records of Achievement initiative is one of a number that have demonstrated what can be achieved by involving students in assessment as part of a learning dialogue with their teacher and requiring them to take more responsibility for their own learning.

However, this and other similar assessment initiatives designed to enhance learning, in the very process of gathering widespread legitimacy and national prominence, have tended to become drained of their original educational purpose. Although as mentioned in Chapter 10, Records of Achievement have now evolved into the very significant 'Progress File' initiative in the UK context, they and related initiatives aimed at incorporating a measure of self-assessment into the accreditation process itself, still struggle with issues of public trust and legitimacy on the one hand and student attitudes on the other. Moreover, they are often perceived by teachers and other staff as an excessive burden (Broadfoot 1998, 2001). Slowly, the research-based messages that we explored in Chapter 5, namely, that this kind of approach to assessment is both practicable and extremely rewarding, are beginning to spread.

However, it would appear to be the case that until such potentially radical assessment initiatives are explicitly underpinned by an understanding of what is to be gained from them and why, in terms of both improved learning and improved motivation to learn, they will not prove robust enough to resist the powerful forces of tradition and the status quo.

Communities of practice

Some of the most innovative thinking about how the insights concerning assessment for learning can be put into practice, centre on recent developments in learning theory itself and the notion of 'communities of practice' (Lave and Wenger 1991). Drawing on socio-cultural approaches to understanding the learning process which emphasize the way in which it is 'situated' in a web of interactions and contextual factors – some social, some psychological – this kind of assessment emphasizes the importance of collaboration and mutual support. Although peer assessment – students being asked to assess each other's work – has been a practical expedient used by teachers since time immemorial, this latest version has considerably more potential to support learning.

The novelty of this perspective on assessment is well-articulated in the following extract drawn from a major contemporary study of how teaching and learning can be transformed. Arguing against the value of traditional, testing-oriented approaches to assessment, James and Brown (2005: 19) suggest that:

> From a socio-cultural perspective ... measures 'of this kind' completely miss the point. If being a learner is about being a member of the community and engaging in norms of social practice and tool use, or if one accepts 'knowledge creation' as an important learning outcome in a knowledge society, then the perceived need for valid and reliable assessment instruments as defined by classical test theory, might disappear. Indeed by definition there is a static quality about the traditional criteria for good quality assessment, which derives mostly from their origin in psychometrics, i.e. the science of measurement, of mental traits that are assumed to be

distinct and relatively stable. If however the learning outcomes in which we are interested are dynamic, shifting and sometimes original or unique, we need a new methodology for assessment, perhaps drawing more on ethnographic and peer-review approaches in social science, appreciation and connoisseurship in the arts, and advocacy, testimony and judgement in law. There are many models (and metaphors) in other fields on which to draw, but the challenges posed by such a 'turn' would of course be enormous in the field of education.

In this perspective, learning is as much about participation as it is about achievement. As such, this call for a radically new assessment perspective echoes very similar and, at the time, very influential, thinking about curriculum development that was prominent in the 1970s. This approach to curriculum development also emphasized the importance of students' active engagement in learning and of collaboration between students; the ceding of a significant degree of ownership and autonomy in learning to the students themselves and an acceptance that learning would produce idiosyncratic, as well as general, outcomes. Significantly, it was the advent of a growing concern with accountability that largely stifled the momentum behind this curriculum movement since the latter was not accompanied by similarly radical ideas about how assessment should change (Stenhouse 1979; Bruner 1986).

Elwood and Klenowski (2002) provide an example of how a 'community of assessment practice' might operate in higher education. They describe a case study of a Masters programme in which they sought to empower students, through the use of peer and self-assessment, to become a community of shared practice.

There are many different kinds of reflection and evaluation which it may be appropriate to include in this respect. As well as students engaging in both formative and summative self-assessment, opportunities for them to engage in peer assessment will increase the possibility of their internalizing assessment criteria and sharing insights. Equally, teachers can reflect on their own teaching and receive evaluative feedback from pupils and students in this respect. At the heart of all such activities is the creation of a community of understanding in relation to assessment criteria and the sharing of the interpretation of these criteria in a climate of mutual trust:

> in pursuing the goals of effective assessment for learning we see it as fundamental for teachers and pupils to grow in a community of practice where nothing in the assessment process is hidden and all hurdles are understood clearly and explicitly. It is only then that assessment will be fully understood as the most important tool for effective learning. (Elwood and Klenowski 2002: 7)

Clearly, no innovation in assessment practice will work unless it is carefully planned and integrated with other aspects of teaching and learning. It is also important that it should not be too ambitious. Small, secure steps are a better basis for changing the culture than attempts to revolutionize whole programmes. These insights into the management of assessment change have been constantly reiterated over many development projects in the last few decades (Broadfoot 2005).

Yet the impact of such innovative assessment approaches continues to be marginal, making little impact on the overwhelming dominance of more conventional forms of assessment. It is not without significance that such approaches have tended to take most firm root in vocational and professional educational provision, rather than in mainstream schooling. One reason for this is the different assessment priorities that prevail in more vocational education and training contexts. In these fields, the emphasis is on developing the appropriate range of skills and knowledge for the occupation in question. Hence the assessment emphasis is on competence, rather than competition, on a criterion-referenced, rather than a norm-referenced, approach.

Moreover, the close link between training and subsequent work performance, reinforces the importance of the validity of the assessment, in comparison with reliability. Initial vocational training is often the first stage in what may be a required programme of Continuing Professional Development (CPD) to update regularly professional skills and knowledge. In these contexts, there is likely to be more awareness of the need to foster the dispositions that will encourage lifelong learning and associated encouragement to use those assessment strategies that are recognized as helping to develop generic learning skills.

Activity 11.3

What skills and attitudes do you think are likely to characterize lifelong learners? How far do current educational practices help to develop these?

Assessment for institutional learning

It is a key argument of this book that what holds true with regard to the assessment of individuals also holds true for the other ways in which assessment is used. The principles of assessment for learning are as applicable to institutional learning as they are to the assessment of learning on the part of individuals and there is now growing enthusiasm for the use of these principles in an institutional context.

The generic sequence of activities associated with assessment for learning is:

- planning (how to achieve objectives or general change);
- doing (learning through the experience of doing with greater awareness);
- recording (thoughts, ideas, experiences, evidence of learning);
- reviewing (reflections on what has happened, making sense of it all);
- evaluating (making judgements about self and own work);
- determining what needs to be done to develop, improve and move on. (Jackson 2001)

These are steps that are clearly applicable to institutions as well where the same continuum exists between traditional summative approaches at one extreme, through to more empowering and dynamic collegial approaches at the other. Once again, the parallels are very clear between this institutional analysis and the same set of arguments pertaining to teachers and students.

Summary

In this part of the book we have presented a good deal of evidence documenting how assessment can be used constructively to support the learning of both individuals and institutions. We have explored why a shift of emphasis is needed, and offered some insights as to how this might be done.

Such assessment requires changes in established teaching and learning practices and, above all, in established assessment practices. It requires a fundamental shift in assessment priorities so that the willingness to apply what is already known about the significant gains to be made by using assessment to support learning overrides other concerns such as 'teaching the test'.

There are at last indications that this route to improving the quality of learning in the classroom may actually now be beginning to become a reality. New assessment techniques are being widely explored by practitioners. These range from the provision of tests online which allows learners to monitor their own learning needs and achievements through to the use of peer assessment and self-assessment including the production of portfolios.

Yet the vast bulk of assessment activity, whether in schools or in universities, continues to be of a more traditional kind in the form of examinations, assessed assignments and practicals resulting in marks and grades. Since these latter continue to be the major elements of 'assessment for communication', they continue to receive the lion's share of institutional resources and of teachers' and students' attention. Indeed, 'trading for grades', question-spotting and all the other paraphernalia of the examination game is probably more in evidence now than it has ever been. Thus although the new assessment approaches now being developed are hardly radical, they are, nevertheless, inherently contradictory.

Thus, for assessment priorities to change in the way described in this chapter will require a fundamental shift of emphasis at the level of both policy and practice. In particular, it will require policy-makers to be willing to build on the powerful insights now emerging from educational research in the field of assessment and learning in setting national educational priorities. The message is in fact a very simple one: Assessment for learning works. Indeed this is one of the very few areas of education where the evidence concerning how to raise standards is clear and unambiguous. The message for policy-makers has been ably summarized by the American assessment expert Rick Stiggins:

- If you wish to appear accountable, test your students.
- If you wish to improve schools, teach teachers to assess their students.
- If you wish to maximize learning, teach students to assess themselves. (Stiggins 2004)

Stiggins' call to arms is as challenging as it is important. It highlights the fundamental tension between the different purposes and priorities for educational assessment that lie at the heart of this book. How might this challenge be addressed and how much does it matter? These questions provide the focus for the final, concluding part of this book.

Key references

Black, P. and Wiliam, D. (2003) *Working Within the Black Box*. London: Kings College.
CERI (2005) *Formative Assessment: Improving learning in secondary classrooms*. Paris: OECD.
Clark, S. (2003) *Enriching Feedback in the Primary Classroom*. London: Hodder and Stoughton.

Useful websites

http://www.qca.org.uk/
This website by the Qualifications and Curriculum Authority (QCA) provides practical guidance and case studies for teachers in the UK on how to use day-to-day assessment effectively to improve teaching and learning.

www.assessmentinst.com/aboutus.php
In the United States, the Assessment Training Institute provides many up-to-date resources for innovative assessment approaches.

Part Five
THE WAY AHEAD

Breaking the Mould 12

In this book I have sought to define what educational assessment is and the part that it plays in relation to individuals, institutions and society. In this concluding section we bring together the perspectives and issues explored in previous chapters to provide the foundation for a vision of assessment for the twenty-first century; a vision that takes into account the profound changes that are happening in the world as a whole, and how these are likely to impact on formal education and wider opportunities for learning in the future. In summarizing the key messages of the analyses presented so far we shall explore the implications they raise for all the partners in learning – learners themselves, teachers, institutions, the community and government.

Empowering Individuals

As we saw in Chapter 5, we live in a time of rapid and global change. Young people growing up today are likely to have at least four careers; they will certainly not have a job for life. Changes in technology grow ever-more rapid with a doubling of computer power every 18 months. Values can no longer simply be passed on from one generation to another. This leaves individuals with the challenge of working out not only their personal identity, in a situation of multiple choices, but also their individual values and morality. Moreover, we live in an age in which the traditional sources of 'ontological security' – trust, predictability and face-to-face associations which are essential to the 'biographic project' (Gibbons 1994: 268) are being eroded:

> in a world of manufactured uncertainty schools have tended to resort to traditional approaches
> to curriculum and pedagogy ... Schools are increasingly caught-up in modes of productivism
> concentrating on producing human, at the expense of social, capital and bracketing out the
> moral equity and ethical issues that do not appear to fit. Yet, as we now see, through ex-
> amples of systemic underachievement and alienation, youth suicide and outbreaks of violence,
> the repressed returns in unfortunate ways as these examples indicate it is not good enough
> that education is reduced to the barren lexicon of economics with a little equity and welfare
> on the side.

Education must move away from 'the full certainty of consensus that such language both suggests and seeks to effect. Education only flourishes in an environment that stimulates new ideas, dissident views, debates and critics in the context of mutual debate and trust' (Cox 1995).

As Cox continues:

> Schools have a key role in building social as well as human capital, of developing trust and se-
> curity but at present they are not well placed to do so being increasingly caught-up in marketized
> and corporatized institutional management and bureaucratized curriculum. Neither contribute
> to educational harmony. Indeed, both have a negative impact on schools' and systems' cap-
> acities to develop social capital and to create the conditions for generative politics. Further,
> both encourage schools to adopt traditional authority relations with young people. In a post-
> traditional society schools cannot assume that the building of trust, mutuality and produc-
> tive risk taking will happen automatically. (p. 272)

Not surprisingly, there is a growing consensus that contemporary models of education are showing signs of strain. The first and most obvious indicator of this is the sheer number of young people emerging from the process of formal education lacking fundamental skills. For example, in England there are 7 million adults, approximately 20 per cent of the adult population, who are functionally illiterate, as in they cannot read direction indicators on buses, menus or supermarket labels. Nor is such illiteracy confined to particular ethnic groups or ages. The levels of illiteracy have remained obstinately constant over the last two decades (Moser 1999); and in 2005 one in six adults did not have the literacy skills expected of an 11-year-old (Leitch 2005).

Figures for the numbers of adults with numeracy problems are worse. Twenty to 25 per cent of adults cannot work out the change they should receive from £2 for two objects purchased for 60p each. Over 5 million people of working age in the UK have no qualification at all. And evidence suggests that illiteracy and innumeracy are the clearest paths to social exclusion.

This is not a problem that is specific to the UK. The problems of underachievement and disaffection are widespread. A recent study in Queensland, Australia, for example, provides graphic illustration of the sources of disaffection being experienced by many of the less successful youngsters in the school system. The perceived irrelevance of a good deal of curriculum content, coupled with their perception of not being treated with respect, has caused many youngsters to turn their back on learning (Pitman 2003).

Clearly there are many potential reasons why individuals emerge from ten or more years of formal schooling without the basic tools to function as adult citizens. A key element, however, is a loss of confidence and self-esteem, which is the experience of many as they go through formal education. Individuals who fail to experience success come to regard themselves as failures as we saw in Chapter 10. This in turn leads to their progressive disillusion with, and disengagement from, an educational process in which they do not experience success, and hence seems increasingly irrelevant.

As if this were not serious enough, people also hold intuitive theories of intelligence and these seem to determine the goals that people set themselves. As Stevenson and Palmer (1994: 132) argue: 'the evidence suggests that intuitive theories and beliefs can interfere with learning and may be resistant to change through explicit tuition'. As we discussed in Chapter 10, such intuitive theories affect the way students interpret their own actions and the views they hold of themselves and of others. They underlie students' self-concepts in a way that determines their motivation to learn and the likelihood that they will attempt to learn at all.

There is a clear message here. For learning to take place in any real sense, individuals must believe that they can be successful in their learning goals and be motivated to pursue them. In the trenchant words of one US psychologist: 'no curricula overhaul, no instructional innovation, no change in school organization, no toughening of standards, no rethinking of teacher training or compensation will succeed if students do not come to school interested in and committed to learning' (Steinberg 1996: 194).

This is not a new *cri de coeur*. Outstanding educators have long recognized that for real learning to take place students must be personally enthused and engaged. As long ago as 1941 Sir Richard Livingston wrote:

> the test of a successful education is not the amount of knowledge that a pupil takes away from a school but his appetite to know and his capacity to learn. If the school sends out children with the desire for knowledge and some idea of how to acquire and use it, it will have done its work. Too many leave school with the appetite killed and the mind loaded with undigested lumps of information. The good schoolmaster (sic) is known by the number of valuable subjects that he declines to teach.

Or, as Albert Einstein put it, even more succinctly: 'Teaching should be such that what is offered is perceived as a valuable gift and not as a hard duty.'

Activity 12.1

Try to list some of the new pressures that are impacting on education today. What implications do you think such pressures have for educational assessment?

Despite these powerful calls for radically different educational priorities, the educational status quo has proved stubbornly resistant to change. What do you think are the main reasons for this?

The Potential of E-Assessment

Although it has proved very difficult for individuals seeking a different approach to education to bring about change on any significant scale, this may be about to change. There are signs today that the stranglehold of tradition may be beginning to loosen as new technologies create the possibility of new ways of thinking, just as they did two centuries ago when educational assessment first became used on a mass scale. We are still in the early stages of the digital technologies that will revolutionize the delivery of education in ways that we cannot yet envisage. But already the advent of interactive technologies of all kinds is making possible a personalized, instant and engaging pedagogy in a way undreamed of even five years ago.

Fundamental to the possibility of change in assessment practices, are the developments that have taken place in recent years in technology. These developments have made possible the advent of 'e-learning' and increasingly, 'e-assessment'. Sophisticated electronic learning platforms, multimedia technologies and wireless communication have made it possible for students to learn remotely, when and where they wish to and – even in some cases – what and how.

Universities have been particularly quick to seize on the new commercial opportunities such developments provide, along with major international companies and even relatively small private providers. 'Flexible' and 'blended' learning for higher and professional courses, as well as a whole range of personal learning needs, are now widely available on an international basis. As such, it opens up a scale of access to high-quality learning opportunities hitherto undreamed of.

If the advent of e-learning represents a hugely significant development in terms of potential access to learning, e-assessment is just as significant. Already it is big business with international testing agencies such as the Educational Testing Service (ETS) in the United States and Cambridge Assessment in the UK – both long-established providers of more traditional forms of summative assessment – developing their international provision of tests and examinations online (McFarlane 2003). On a smaller scale, individual institutions and individual teachers are now also increasingly able to use technology to test their own students 'online'.

But perhaps most fundamental of all in this respect, are the changing skills and attitudes of the students themselves. The current 'twitch-speed' generation is growing up with fundamentally different ways of working and knowing to previous generations who are now, by contrast, generally 'digital peasants' (Prensky 2003). Young people's familiarity with computer games in particular has taught them high-speed decision-making and constant reflection on their own learning as they apply and reapply appropriate tactics and strategies for success – something lacking in many formal education contexts. Every move is recorded, and every second provides useful feedback on that move. The player must become adept at self-assessment and at understanding their own strengths and weaknesses, striving always to improve their personal best and reflecting after the game on the basis of the scores achieved.

Games provide opportunities for 'ipsative' assessment in seeing if you can beat your personal best, formative feedback that lets you know whether you are improving and summative testing when this is sought, leading players to reflect constantly on their own learning as they decide their choice of tactics and strategies. This is very much in the spirit of self-assessment discussed in Chapter 11.

In short, games, as teachers have long recognized, are excellent learning tools in that they are interactive, provide rapid feedback, opportunities for extensive practice, engagement with intellectual complexity, emotional involvement and, increasingly, open-ended outcomes that challenge the creativity of the player. They train the player in the skills of metacognition; they introduce the player to issues of strategy, train them to harness concentration and develop social skills as well as introducing more subtle issues of morality and ethics. In short, games, particularly the electronic games available today, demonstrate how effective the right kind of assessment can be in supporting learning.

Games also provide striking evidence of the disjuncture between the avidly pursued opportunities of the digital world and the all too often reluctant engagement of the traditional classroom. They provide a clear message that the world of education needs to recognize the changes taking place in the perspectives, skills and experiences of today's students and the opportunities that increasingly exist to implement the lessons of this book concerning assessment using the potential of ICT. Assessment that builds confidence by being personalized and engaging and recognizing the link between the cognitive and the affective; that provides substantive and immediate feedback; that can cover the full range of learning objectives; that is available on demand and is efficient, accessible and, potentially, collaborative.

E-assessment also provides an unparalleled opportunity for diagnostic assessment in making possible evidence of the problem-solving processes a learner has used, rather than assessing outcomes alone. It makes readily possible too, more tailored assessment tasks which accompany individualized learning routes through a body of material. Thus each learner can progress in relation to their own needs and interests and, potentially, even in relation to their own preferred learning style.

E-assessment also provides the possibility of 'just-in-time' assessment which, like production processes, is available on demand when the student feels ready. In the past, such 'on-demand' assessment has been largely confined to private activities such as music and sport assessments, but even in these contexts, the tests have necessarily been organized as specific events to be prepared for, anticipated and feared just like more conventional external examinations and tests. By contrast, online tests such as the UK driving licence theory test, or many foreign language tests, are available for a fee at test centres at virtually any time.

Already, e-assessment is demonstrating its capacity to address the learning process itself rather than its products alone through, for example, problem-solving, as well as e-portfolios, open-web examinations, authentic foreign language tests, analysis of spoken arguments and debates and the assessment of group work. Moreover, there are likely to be rapid and wide-ranging developments in such techniques in the near future, bringing with them the potential for greatly increased quality of assessment in terms of validity, reliability and utility while significantly increasing efficiency.

The advent of these new interactive technologies thus represents a major opportunity for a fundamental change in assessment practice. As formative assessment in the classroom, e-assessment is likely to become rapidly 'A-learning' – assessment for learning which is rooted in the process of rapid and regular feedback that the computer makes possible.

'A-learning' readily provides the kind of personalized, engaging and constructivist learning opportunity which, as we have seen, is fundamental to motivating learners. As such it responds to both the cognitive and the affective dimensions of learning. It builds confidence and, as the world of computer games so clearly demonstrates, it builds hunger for more. By fragmenting the assessment process, it reduces the negative impact of 'categoric' assessment, translating the crude language of levels and grades into a more fluid and developmental narrative.

Moreover, by providing substantive and immediate feedback, it is both efficient and of immense value in tutoring the learner's ability to reflect and plan for the future. Through the use of simulations, it is increasingly able to provide for more 'authentic' assessments of performance so allowing the full range of learning objectives to be addressed. This means that the assessments can have high levels of validity without a corresponding loss of reliability. Last, but not least, such assessment lends itself to the collaboration which, as we have seen, is such a key feature of good learning opportunities and which traditional, essentially individualist, forms of assessment have done so much to inhibit. 'A-learning' offers a 'community of practice' which, as we discussed in Chapter 11, is in the best traditions of apprenticeship learning, albeit on a simulated basis.

We may summarize these characteristics of 'A-learning' as follows:

- personalized
- confidence-building

- constructive
- engaging
- providing substantive and immediate feedback
- covering the full range of learning objectives
- combining formative and summative assessment
- available on demand
- combining effective and cognitive learning dimensions
- potentially collaborative
- reducing the power of categorization through greater fragmentation
- sequential
- networked
- efficient
- accessible in a range of modes.

This is a brave vision indeed. Meanwhile, for 'digital natives', the contrast between the rich, exciting, rewarding and personalized world of digital media and the relatively drab authoritarian, generalized delivery of traditional forms of pedagogy is increasingly marked. For while the opportunity to take advantage of these benefits will be increasingly widely available, its realization in formal educational settings, both through ICT and in more conventional forms of assessment, depends to a considerable extent on the kind of fundamental change in our thinking about assessment that has been the subject of this book. It will require us to 'put the kids before the content and there is something even more important than the kids, the spark. Why do we need the spark (i.e. engagement) so badly? It is not attention deficit. "I am just not listening"' (Prensky 2003). While content, rather than kids, remains the principal focus of education, the vision is unlikely to be fulfilled.

To summarize then: We have a situation in which individuals feel engaged and challenged, to a greater or lesser extent, by conventional forms of education. Some are motivated by the promise of extrinsic rewards such as praise and high marks; some are more willing to conform; and many, either less successful or less conformist students, find the experience more or less damaging. Moreover, as has been argued throughout this book, it is assessment that shapes the specification of curriculum and learning outcomes. It is assessment that defines what constitutes achievement. It is assessment that represents the hurdles individuals perceive they have to jump and it is assessment that strikes at the heart of an individual's feelings.

In short, 'many individuals are uncertain when faced with formal learning, they lack personal confidence, they are easily dissuaded, they have often been failed by formal education before' (Browning 2000). To be successful, learners need to develop their sense of self-esteem, their sense of having the power within themselves to change their situations if they so wish, and the realization that exercising that power involves increasing their knowledge and understanding. We, therefore, need to put the issue of motivation consciously and deliberately at the heart of the educational process.

Activity 12.2

Prepare two lists, one of the advantages of traditional forms of assessment and one of the advantages of e-assessment. To what conclusions does a comparison of the two lists lead you in terms of what could and should be done on the one hand, and what is likely to be done, on the other?

Refocusing Goals

If the first plank in understanding the nature of the new vision for education needed for the twenty-first century is the recognition of the key importance of individual confidence and motivation, the second, which is closely associated with this, is the focus of the learning itself. As we saw in Chapter 5, in recent years there has been a great deal of discussion around the concept of key skills – sometimes called 'work-related skills' or 'transferable skills' – since there is now an increasingly widespread consensus that students need to be equipped, with 'life skills' or 'key skills'. These typically include communication skills, numeracy, ICT skills, working in teams, problem-solving, and even 'emotional intelligence' – the capacity to understand other people's emotions and to manage one's own. Crucially such lists also typically include learning how to learn and the skills of reflection and managing one's own performance and future learning.

Such educational objectives are a long way from the traditional curriculum fare of knowledge and understanding and other cognitive learning outcomes. They are rooted partly in recognition of the kinds of challenges which will face tomorrow's citizens, but also in the growing literature on the nature of learning itself. By the same token, assessment priorities will need to change from the traditional domination of its role in selection and prediction, to a greater focus on the certification of achievement and its use to stimulate learning and empower learners.

It is clear that there are many straws in the wind concerning more or less fundamental change in assessment. Changes in the goals of education, in the means for delivering it and in our understanding of how to make it most effective, are combining to challenge the professional community as never before to rethink its priorities. It has been argued that the growth of interest in new forms of assessment is part of a more general shift from scientism to a more postmodernist acceptance of relativity, fuzziness and with it, a more humanistic perspective (Gipps 1995). Positivism is giving way to phenomenology in the sense that it is increasingly being recognized that assessment is inevitably a humanistic project because it involves multiple actions by human beings.

Unfortunately, the progressive politicization of assessment activity that this book has documented, underpins a tendency to gloss over the inevitable relativities of assessment in the pursuit of political legitimacy and defensibility. The notions of objectivity and rigour that are frequently articulated by politicians and policy-makers to enhance public credibility, obscures what each one of us, as an individual, knows from our own experience. Namely, that assessment is a more or less blunt instrument which often misses its target and all too often causes significant damage. The quest for the 'holy grail' of objective educational measurement is every bit as ephemeral as the rather more celebrated quest for the 'holy grail' itself. Both quests have typically been 'high-stakes' and ended in dead-ends; both are expensive and arcane; both have resulted in huge suffering while being doomed to failure since the object of the quest is itself a myth.

But if the price of the grail myth has been high in human terms, it is nothing compared to the educational cost of the 'myth of measurement' (Broadfoot 1996b). The obsessive search for educational measurement accuracy as the basis for prediction and selection has lead to a separation between the two pillars of learning, namely, assessment and instruction. The reification of educational assessment has underpinned the overwhelming tendency to value what is measurable rather than measuring what is valued.

Thus, in Chapter 4 it was argued that as the twenty-first century dawns, the educational world finds itself in thrall to an outdated technology largely propped up by political expediency. This situation tends to preclude a more fundamental examination of the fitness for purpose of assessment in terms of its impact on learners and their families, the pursuit of the skills sought by employers; the levels of human capital sought by governments; the accuracy of selection devices and the encouragement to lifelong learning. Rather, as we argued in Chapter 4, around the world, the headlong pursuit of qualifications and competitive advantage creates an examination rat race which drives out virtually all other goals of education and schooling. As one commentator has put it:

> assessment – more precisely examination – is rapidly becoming the sole objective so it would seem of education … Increasingly, our education system at all levels is succumbing to the pernicious doctrine … a pestilence caught exclusively off managerial moguls. Emotional enfeeblement and moral degeneration could become the defining characteristics of our society by the turn of the century as today's school children take on the executive role. Those of us who resist the march of the assessors do so on the grounds that the loss of happiness is too high a price to pay for a spurious legitimacy. (Ross 1986: 9)

Children in England today are the most tested generation there has ever been. They are subjected to some 200 different testing episodes as they go through school, starting in the infant years and repeating every year relentlessly as a diet of summative and increasingly high-stakes assessment. In UK schools alone, 20 million examination scripts are marked each year containing some 2 billion answers and involving some 50,000 markers (Roan 2003). The cost of this obsession with testing is very considerable both for individuals as we saw in Chapter 5 and in terms of the human and financial resources involved.

Enduring Dilemmas

At the heart of this scenario, is a technology that was invented as part of the hugely significant economic and political developments of the nineteenth century. This was a time, as I argued in Chapter 2, when selection and prediction functions became paramount. Since then, there have been successive attempts to break the mould which shaped educational assessment at that time. In Chapter 11, for example, I discussed the significance of the powerful Records of Achievement movement in the UK as well as significant developments in the use of continuous assessment and, more recently, portfolio assessment.

In the United States the backlash against so-called 'objective' testing using multiple-choice tests was associated with the pursuit of 'authentic' assessment in which the aim was to incorporate a greater measure of validity by designing an assessment task more like the real-life situation (Koretz et al. 1998). The world of vocational education, in particular, has seen a resurgence of interest in the assessment of competency (Gonczi 1993). Most recent of all, as we saw in Chapter 10, has been the explosion of interest in the capacity of assessment to make learning itself more effective by enthusing and empowering learners of all ages and stages.

Until recently, however, all such developments, as this book has made clear, have been bedevilled by the ongoing need for traditional forms of summative assessment, particularly written tests as the basis for certification and selection, by the continued application of what the American Academy of Science describes as twentieth-century statistics applied to nineteenth-century psychology (cited by Black 2001). But although it has been widely recognized – as we saw in Chapter 4 – that the pursuit of traditional forms of assessment is deeply constraining and often counter-productive, the need for an acceptable mechanism for certifying particular levels of achievement and on the basis of which selection decisions can be made, has seemed to be overwhelming.

Chapter 7's exploration of 'the quality agenda' documented how this stranglehold has been further strengthened by the enthusiastic use of student examination data by governments in order to evaluate the quality of institutions and systems. Thus traditional assessment approaches have continued to predominate.

This is the situation in which the world of education finds itself today, on the cusp between a real opportunity for change and the powerful forces of conservatism. Whether such change is likely and how it might come about is the subject of the final, more speculative chapter of this book

Key references

Prensky, M. (2001). *On the Horizon*. NCB University Press, Volume 9, Number 5 (October).

Prensky, M. (2003) *Beyond the Exam: Innovative approaches to learning and assessment.* Bristol: Futurelab.

Stevenson, R. J. and Palmer, J. A. (1994) *Learning: Principles, processes and practices.* London: Cassell.

Useful websites

www.becta.org.uk

A UK government agency (British Educational Communication and Technology Agency) promoting the use of information and communications technology; site includes news, projects and resources on lifelong and special education including new approaches to assessment based around the use of new technologies.

www.ceoforum.org/downloads/report4.pdf

A US site that seeks to align student assessment with educational objectives that include twenty-first-century skills given that since 2003, every US state should be matching assessment to the new standards that include such skills.

www.marcprensky.com/blog

Marc Prensky's Weblog provides many examples of Prensky's approach including:

Finally, Some Kids! Project Inkwell Update. A Great Vision of Technology and Learning. Digital Natives, Digital Immigrants: Origins of Terms. The Prensky Challenge.

www.unesco.org/education/educprog/tve/nseoul/docse/rstratve.html

This a website linked to UNESCO that links counselling techniques; career, educational and labour-market information to new assessment approaches.

13 Seeing the World Anew

No problem can be solved from the same consciousness that created it. We must learn to see the world anew. Albert Einstein

The Pervasive Power of Assessment

Throughout this book we have been exploring the different purposes that educational assessment serves and the very real tensions that these give rise to. One of the key arguments has been about the need for greater clarity in our thinking about assessment to ensure that, as far as possible, the procedures we are using are the most suitable for the task in question. Ensuring 'fitness for purpose' and, hence, quality means that all those involved in education, from policy-makers to practitioners and even students themselves and their parents, must become a great deal more 'assessment literate' than has typically been the case up to now.

This book has highlighted a situation in which, despite the fact that the tentacles of educational assessment powerfully affect all aspects of education and training in every country of the world, societies around the globe have been more or less content not to question the status quo. At best, they have sought to tinker with it at the margins. Yet, as we saw in Chapter 2, the evidence suggests that, even in their own terms, more traditional forms of assessment are far from perfect in providing infallible judgements of student performance. Because educational assessment is essentially a human activity, which involves social interaction and judgement, it is inevitably a rough-and-ready process, subject to all the vagaries of values and perception that characterize people's behaviour. Postmodern perspectives are now challenging the dominance of science and its assumptions of objectivity, allowing the recognition that perhaps the best basis for judgement is that of 'multiple subjectivities' – the combined judgements of a number of different assessors. This is already widely accepted in the world of sport and artistic performance.

This is not to say that the attempt to provide rigorous, dispassionate assessment of achievement is not a good thing. Clearly this would be nonsense in a world where the need to communicate achievement through qualifications and to provide the fairest possible basis for selection continues unabated. It is rather to argue for a more sophisticated and well-informed approach to assessment so that both some of its unnecessarily damaging consequences are minimized and that its potential to contribute positively to learning is maximized.

Educational assessment is a technology as powerful in its own way as any of the most pervasively influential inventions that have impacted on our planet to date. It is certainly as significant as the steam engine and the computer; it may even be as significant as the invention of the wheel. Though at first sight this may seem a ludicrous claim, the fact that educational assessment shapes the school experience of every child in the world, is a very important reality. It is educational assessment that shapes parents' priorities as they seek a good future for their children; it is educational assessment that shapes teachers' priorities and curriculum content; it is educational assessment that governs students' orientation to their learning and it is educational assessment that is a powerful tool in the hands of policy-makers for controlling the educational system as a whole and for appeasing voters.

Those things that are relatively easy to assess get taught. Those that are not are increasingly neglected. As is often said, what counts is what is measured; what is measured is not necessarily what counts. In the face of the relentless advance of educational assessment, the spiritual, the moral, the creative, the social – even the physical – have fallen victim to the lack of techniques to assess them.

The academic and the cognitive skills that underpin learning have, hence, come to dominate our contemporary notions of what education is and should be for. So profound is this domination, that it is almost impossible to imagine an alternative. Yet imagine we must, for the world is changing and there are new priorities. Educational assessment in its current forms represents a dangerous source of inertia on the capacity of education systems to respond to the consequences of the fundamental economic, technological and social changes that are now impacting on an increasingly global society.

A Call to Arms

Thus, this chapter is a call to arms; a call to recognize the need for change in our educational, and hence our assessment, priorities; the need to challenge the dominance of measurement issues in our thinking about assessment; a call to use the considerable knowledge that is already available to us about the nature of the educational changes that will be needed and how assessment can best support these.

As we discussed in Chapter 5, we are entering what is popularly referred to as 'the learning age' or 'the knowledge society'. It will require both more and better learning. It will require mass engagement in lifelong learning if people are to keep pace with rapidly changing technologies and the constant need for new skills. Individuals can no longer anticipate a job, or even a career, 'for life'. Nor will there be a ready-made consensus around values. It will, therefore, require changes in curriculum and teaching methods as well as in assessment if we are to change students' orientation to learning.

There have already been many attempts to conceive an appropriate curriculum model for the future which reflects these imperatives (Bayliss 2000). In their inspiring book *Towards Schooling for the 21st Century*, for example, Dalin and Rust (1996) review a variety of government initiatives from Norway to New Zealand that recognize the changes that are needed and the new types of learning that will be appropriate for the societies of the future. The four elements of their own model – 'culture, others, myself, nature' – echo many of the arguments of this book in stressing the need for a wider range of knowledge and skills and, crucially, different ways of engaging with the learning process.

But for such curriculum frameworks to be translated into reality in the classroom will require changes in the way in which we think about assessment and, particularly, in how we think about accountability and 'the quality agenda'. It will be necessary to ensure that the various different purposes of assessment are addressed as a whole so they are as complementary to each other as possible, despite the inevitable tensions that we identified in Chapter 4.

The challenge to accepted models of education is thus of the most fundamental kind. It is on the same scale as that which confronted the governments of a different era faced with the challenge of providing schooling for the masses for the first time. The result was the invention of an elementary school system that could provide the rudiments of literacy and numeracy for all. Another invention at that time was the idea of formal educational assessment. The evolution of current assessment technologies over a century or more started with the need to provide a defensible and rational means of identifying the relative success or failure of individual learners. But, as we saw in Chapter 3, this technology rapidly developed into a 'technology of control'.

It is the combined weight of these two policy agendas of selection and control that makes the current assessment technology so hard for governments to change. Nevertheless, if governments want to make a serious impact on the quality of learning, they will have to be prepared to take risks even if, at present: 'The red flag carriers do not want a learning train; they would prefer a faster horse. They talk of adapting existing models of education rather than looking for new ones' (Lucas 1999: 19).

Thus in the final part of this chapter, we consider briefly how this might be done.

Towards Responsible Assessment

The message concerning how current models of education and its assessment need to change is a deceptively simple one. It is that we need to prioritize relationships and engagement. We need to give learners more autonomy and to provide more opportunities for collaboration between students and teachers if we are to help students develop their generic learning skills. We need to give learners rapid and substantive feedback and to be sensitive to the emotional charge of both assessment and learning. All this is perfectly feasible. There are two major stumbling blocks, however.

The first of these concerns the politicization of assessment. Established assessment practices enjoy considerable public trust. Any attempt to change them, even in a less than radical way, is likely to result in a storm of protest. As experience around the world has demonstrated, it would be a brave politician who attempted it.

The second stumbling block concerns the continuing use of assessment as a rationing device for scarce opportunities. The annual scramble to gain entry to the best schools and, particularly, the best universities, shows no sign of diminishing. It is, if anything, getting worse as it becomes an increasingly global competition.

Thus any serious attempt to change the status quo regarding assessment and so liberate education to be able to respond to changing priorities, must address these realities. In what follows, I suggest some 'dos' and 'don'ts' that should guide future thinking with regard to assessment that are both practicable and achievable within the current context.

Dos and Don'ts of a New Assessment Regime

Dos

- Put learning first;
- Keep assessment for selection to a minimum;
- Recognize the powerful positive potential of assessment as a means of supporting learning;
- Ensure teachers of all kinds have high levels of knowledge and understanding regarding assessment;

- Train students in the art of assessment so they can become skilled in managing their own learning;
- Invest actively in the development of new assessment techniques which are appropriate for twenty-first-century learning goals;
- Recognize the many undesirable side-effects of much contemporary assessment practice;
- Elevate fitness for purpose as a key assessment 'health check';
- Build on the research evidence that exists regarding 'what works' rather than custom and practice;
- Recognize that learning is as much about feelings as it is about 'brains' or intellect and act accordingly.

Don'ts

- Use student assessment data as an instrument to encourage competition through league tables of institutional performance;
- Do to children, and all those pursuing formal courses of study in education institutions, what you would not like done to you;
- Pursue assessment approaches that are almost exclusively individual when so much of learning is a socially collaborative activity;
- Pretend to be unaware of the rough-and-ready nature of conventional assessment results but rather use these intelligently in conjunction with other sources of insight;
- Waste huge amounts of time and money on educational assessment that does no good and often does a lot of harm.

To move towards a new set of priorities in the purposes of assessment and enhanced understanding concerning how it may be harnessed properly to support the educational priorities of the twenty-first century, will require a significant change in the contemporary context. It will, for example, require government to be prepared to do without the crude performance indicators currently used to indicate educational quality. It will require a willingness on the part of governments around the world to accept a less homogeneous language of comparison in exchange for much greater engagement and productivity in educational institutions. It will require society, and those responsible for making selection decisions, to be more willing to recognize forms of qualification built on apparently less robust methodologies of judgement than the traditional written examination. In place of the narrowly focused exam will have to come the multiple subjectivities of observation and interactions of various kinds including electronic transcripts.

There is clearly a very long way to go in moving towards such a vision. However, the vital first step is to recognize the need for change and the possibilities that now exist for this to happen. In a world increasingly characterized by the impact of new technologies, building on the potential offered by these developments represents an unprecedented opportunity to 'see the world anew'.

As we saw in Chapter 2, from its earliest beginnings, educational assessment has had two fundamental characteristics: to enhance learning – what I termed 'assessment for curriculum'; and to recognize achievement – what I termed 'assessment for communication'. The way in which assessment is used will reflect the particular needs of a society at a given stage of development. It will also reflect the prevailing 'zeitgeist' that is a product of particular cultural traditions, ideology and technologies. As society changes, therefore, so will educational assessment. Thus the transition from 'premodern' to 'modern' society, from traditionalist to positivist modes of thinking, underpinned the invention of both modern education systems and technologies for mass assessment.

Today, many would argue that we find ourselves at the interface between the modern and the postmodern eras, when the overwhelming faith in science to solve the world's problems is being called into question. There is arguably a growing recognition that the solutions to the world's problems are likely to be as much human, as they are technical; social, as much as scientific. The zeitgeist is beginning to change.

Contemporary debates around educational assessment are part of this larger movement. Still preoccupied with the search for foolproof methods of judging merit, we nevertheless increasingly recognize the undesirable side-effects of such technologies: the social tensions and individual suffering they produce; the waste of valuable and finite human resources; the pollution of the social world with 'performativity'. As with other technologies, governments find themselves torn between the perceived benefits of the widespread use of established technologies and the growing evidence concerning their undesirable impact. Just as the demands of industry and the creation of jobs must be set against growing evidence about the dangers of global warming and pollution-generated diseases, so the political capital of talking tough about tests and targets must be set against the growing evidence of demoralization, curriculum constraint and the inhibition of lifelong learning.

The Way Forward?

The answer, if there is one in the short term, is quite simply for all levels of the education system to generate a willingness to engage with the evidence – to be *responsible* – in the way they use assessment; for teachers and policy-makers, parents and students, academics and educational evangelists to come together in a consideration of the 'dark alleys and blind bends' (Broadfoot 2005) which have characterized so much educational assessment practice in the past. The need now is for each of these groups to draw on their own painful, personal memories to encourage them to recognize the tremendous emotional impact of assessment, often in the long term as well as the short term; to take seriously the scale of the opportunity for raising standards that good, formative assessment presents for both individuals; and for institutions and for governments to resist the seductive attractions of monitoring that is punitive rather than diagnostic. We need to 'test smarter', rather than test harder.

Above all, we need urgently to recognize the new possibilities that 'A-learning' is opening up which will increasingly render obsolete the familiar distinction between learning and assessment. For summative purposes too, e-assessment offers the promise of rigorous, adaptable, cheap and timely certification as well as comprehensive national monitoring. The need for rationing educational opportunities is likely progressively to diminish as the finite capacity of physical institutions is replaced by the potentially unlimited capacities of online learning. By the same token, the priority for summative assessment is likely to switch back from selection to its more traditional role of certifying achievement.

This is a brave vision of a tapestry of lifelong learning in which individuals are both equipped and motivated to take advantage of a complex web of complementary educational and assessment opportunities. As we have seen in this book, we are very far from this reality at present. The legacy of history and exigency lies like a dead weight on the world's education systems. It is a weight that seems almost impossible to shift at the present time. If anything, the grip of traditional forms of assessment is tightening. Nevertheless, the last decade or so has seen significant developments in our understanding of the way in which assessment can work to either support or inhibit learning. It has also seen unparalleled change in our technical capacity to deliver assessment in ways that could provide a far better balance between the various functions that assessment fulfils for individuals, for institutions and for society. The door is open. We only need to go through it.

References

Abbott, J. (1998) 'Why Good Schools Alone Will Never Be Enough' *The Journal of the 21st Century Learning Initiative* (March). Letchworth, Herts, UK.

Abbott, J. (1999) 'Battery Hens of Free Range Chickens: What kind of education for what kind of world?' *The Journal of the 21st Century Learning Initiative* (January), pp. 1–12. Letchworth, Herts, UK.

Able, G. (2002) 'Testing Times for a Broad Education' *The Times* (28 June).

Airasian, P. W. (1998) 'Symbolic Validation: The case of state mandated high-stakes testing' *Education Evaluation and Policy Analysis* Volume 10, Number 4, pp. 301–15.

Alexander, R. (2000) *Culture and Pedagogy* Oxford: Blackwell.

Almond, D. (1999) *The Times* (15 July), p. 12.

Askey, S. (ed.) (2000) *Feedback for Learning* London: RoutledgeFalmer.

Assessment Reform Group (ARG) (1999) *Assessment for Learning: Beyond the black box* (http: www.assessment-reform-group.org.uk).

Assessment Reform Group (ARG) (2002) *Assessment for Learning: 10 principles* (http: www.assessment-reform-group.org.uk).

Atkins, M., Beattie, J. and Dockrell, B. (1993) *Assessment Issues in Higher Education* Sheffield: Employment Department.

Atkinson, A. and Gregg, P. (2004) 'Selective Education: Who benefits from grammar schools?' *CMPO: Market and Public Organisation* Issue 11 (Autumn), pp. 1–2.

Bakker, S. and Wolf, A. (eds) (2001) 'Examinations and Entry to University: Pressure and change in a mass system' *Assessment in Education* Volume 8, Number 3 (November).

Bandura, A. (1977) *Social Learning Theory* Englewood Cliffs, NJ: Prentice Hall.

Bayliss, V. (2000) *What Should Our Children Learn? Issues around a new curriculum* London: RSA.

Bell, D. (2004) Press release on 'A New Relationship with Schools' OFSTED/DfES.

Bennett, N., Dunne, E. and Carey, C. (2000) *Skills Development in Higher Education and Employment* Buckingham: Society for Research into Higher Education and Open University Press.

Berliner, W. (2003) *The Guardian*, p. 2.

Black, P. (1993) 'Beyond the Exam' conference paper, Association of Assessment Inspectors and Advisers. Reported in *TES* (1 October).

Black, P. (2000) 'Research and the Development of Educational Assessment' *Oxford Review of Education* Volume 26, Numbers 3 and 4, pp. 407–21.

Black, P. (2003) 'Assessment for learning-lessons from research and from practice' Presentation at Beyond Exams conference, 19 November 2003, Bristol.

Black, P. (2001) 'Developing Classroom Formative Assessment' seminar presentation, Bristol University (March).

Black, P., Harrison, C., Lee, C., Marshall, B. and Wiliam, D. (2003) *Assessment for Learning* Maidenhead: Open University Press.

Black, P. and Wiliam, D. (1998) 'Assessment and Classroom Learning' *Assessment in Education* Volume 5, Number 1, pp. 7–74.

Black, P. and Wiliam, D. (2003) *Working Within the Black Box* London: Kings College.

Black, P. and Wiliam, D. (2005) 'Lessons from Around the World: How policies, politics and cultures constrain and afford assessment practices' *The Curriculum Journal* Volume 16, Number 2, pp. 249–61.

Blanchard, J. (2002) *Teaching and Targets: Self-evaluation and school improvement* London: RoutledgeFalmer.

Boekaerts, M. (2002) *Motivation to Learn* Educational Practices, series 10 Geneva: International Academy of Education.

Bonnet, G. (2004) 'Evaluation of Education in the European Union: Policy and methodology' *Assessment in Education* Volume 11, Number 2 (July), pp. 179–93.

Boud, D. (1993) Developing Student Antonomy in Learning. London: Kogan Page.

Boud, D. (2002) 'Sustainable Assessment: Re-thinking assessment for the learning society' *Studies in Continuing Education* Volume 22, Number 2, pp. 151–67.

Boud, D. and Falchikov, N. (1989) 'Student self-assessment in higher education; a meta-analysis' in *Review Educational Research* Vol. 59, no. 4, pp. 395–430.

Boud, D. and Falchikov, N. (2004) 'Beyond Formative and Summative Assessment: Developing a new agenda for assessment for lifelong learning' paper, Assessment 2004 'Beyond Intuition', the second bi-annual joint Northumbria EARLISIG Assessment Conference, University of Bergen, Norway (June 23–25).

Boyle, D. (2001) *The Tyranny of Numbers* London: Harper Collins.

Boyle, D. (2001) 'Things Must Be Static to Be Counted: But life isn't still' *The Observer Review* (14 January), pp. 1–2.

Broadfoot, P. (1979) 'Communication in the Classroom: A study of the role of assessment in motivation' *Educational Review* Volume 31, Number 1, pp. 3–10.

Broadfoot, P. (1989) 'Towards Curssessment: The symbiotic relationship between curriculum and assessment' in Entwistle, N. et al (eds) *Handbook of Educational Ideas and Practices* London: Routledge.

Broadfoot, P. (1990) 'Cinderella and the Ugly Sisters: An assessment policy pantomime in two acts' *The Curriculum Journal* Volume 1, Number 2 (September), pp. 199–215.

Broadfoot, P. (1996a) 'Do We Need to Write It All Down: Managing the challenge of national assessment at KS1 and KS2' in Croll, P. (ed.) *Teachers, Pupils and Primary Schooling* London: Cassell.

Broadfoot, P. (1996b) 'Educational Assessment: The Myth of Measurement' inaugural lecture in Woods, P. (ed.) *Contemporary Issues in Teaching and Learning* Buckingham: Open University Press.

Broadfoot, P. (1996c) *Education, Assessment and Society* Buckingham: Open University Press.

Broadfoot, P. (1998) 'Quality, Standards and Control in Higher Education: What price life-long learning?' *International Studies in Sociology of Education* Volume 8, Number 2, pp. 155–80.

Broadfoot, P. (1998) 'Records of Achievement and The Learning Society: A tale of two discourses' *Assessment in Education* Volume 5, Number 3, pp. 447–77.

Broadfoot, P. (2000) 'Assessment and Intuition' in Atkinson, T. and Claxton, G. (eds) *The Intuitive Practitioner* Buckingham: Open University Press.

Broadfoot, P. (2001) 'Empowerment or Performativity? English assessment policy in the late twentieth century' in Phillips, R. and Furlong, J. (eds) *Education Reform and the State: Twenty-five years of politics, policy and practice* London: RoutledgeFalmer.

Broadfoot, P. (2003) 'Thinking About Feeling: Transforming learning through assessment' invited keynote address, Challenges and Issues in Educational Evaluation Conference, University of the West Indies/ Caribbean Examinations Council, Barbados.

Broadfoot, P. (2005) 'Dark Alleys and Blind Bends: Testing the Language of Learning' *Language Testing* Volume 22, Number 2, pp. 123–41.

Broadfoot, P., James, M., McMeeking, S., Nuttall, D. and Stierer, B. (1984) *Records of Achievement: Report of the National Evaluation of Pilot Schemes* London: HMSO.

Broadfoot, P., Osborn, M., Planel, C. and Pollard, A. (1996) 'Assessment in French Primary Schools' *The Curriculum Journal* Volume 7, Number 2 (Summer), pp. 227–46.

Broadfoot, P., Osborn, M., Planel, C., Sharp, K. and Ward, B. (2000) *Promoting Quality in Learning: Has England got the answer?* London: Cassell.

Broadfoot, P. and Pollard, A. (2000) 'The Changing Discourse of Assessment Policy: The case of English primary education' in Filer, A. (ed.) *Assessment: Social Practice and Social Product* London: Falmer Press.

Brown, M. (1999) 'Problems of Interpreting International Comparative Data' in Jaworski, B. and Phillips, D. (eds) 'Comparing Standards Internationally' *Oxford Studies in Comparative Education* Volume 9, Number 1, pp. 183–207.

Browning, D. (2000) 'What Motivates People to Learn?' seminar paper Goodison Group, Guildford, Surrey.

Bruner, G. (1986) *Actual Minds: Possible worlds* London: Harvard University Press.

Bryant, S., Lam, T., Timmins, A. and Williams, A. (2003) *Formative Assessment for Learning: An annotated bibliography* Hong Kong Institute of Education, Hong Kong, mimeo.

Burgess, S., Propper, C. and Wilson, D. (2003) *Choice: Will more choice improve outcomes in education and healthcare – the evidence from economic research* CMPO: Bristol University.

Carr, M. (2004) *Assessment for Learning: Early childhood examples* New Zealand: Ministry of Education.

Carr, M. and Claxton, G. (2002) 'Tracking the Development of Learning Dispositions' *Assessment in Education* Volume 9, Number 1, pp. 9–39.

CERI (2005) *Formative Assessment: Improving learning in secondary classrooms* Paris: OECD.

Chan, K. (2006) 'Autonomy or Control? Implementing a staff appraisal scheme in higher education in Hong Kong' ed.d dissertation, University of Bristol.

Christie, A. (1968) *Chinese Mythology* London: Paul Hamlyn.

Clark, D. (1994) 'Targets and Target-Related Assessments: Hong Kong's curriculum and assessment project in school based and external assessments' proceedings, 1993 IAEA Conference Mauritius Examinations Syndicate, p. 36.

Clarke, S. (2001) *Unlocking Formative Assessment: Practical Strategies for Enhancing Pupils' Learning in the Primary Classroom* London: Hodder and Stoughton.

Clarke, S. (2003) *Enriching Feedback in the Primary Classroom* London: Hodder and Stoughton.

Claxton, G. (1989) 'Cognition Doesn't Matter if You're Scared, Depressed or Bored' in Adey, P., Bliss, J. and Shayer, M. (eds) *Adolescent Development and School Science* London: Falmer Press.

Claxton, G. (1999) *Wise-up: The challenge of life-long learning* Basingstoke: Picador.

Claxton, G. (2002) *Building Learning Power* Bristol: TLO Ltd.

Coffield, F. (ed.) (1999) *Thinking Truth to Power* Bristol: The Policy Press.

Crooks, T. (1988) 'The Impact of Classroom Evaluation Practices on Students' *Review of Educational Research* Volume 58, Number 4 (Winter), pp. 438–81.

Crooks, T. (2001) 'The Validity of Formative Assessments' British Educational Research Association Conference, Leeds (September).

Csikszentmihalyi, M. K. et al. (1993) *The Roots of Success and Failure* Cambridge: Cambridge University Press.

Cumming, J. (2001) 'Valuing Learning and Learners: The forgotten dimensions of educational assessment worth remembering for the 21st century' IAEA Conference, Brazil.

Dalin, P. and Rust, V. (1996) *Towards Schooling for the 21st Century* London: Cassell.

Dann, R. (2002) *Promoting Assessment as Learning: Improving the Learning Process* London: RoutledgeFalmer.

Daugherty, R. (1995) *National Curriculum Assessment: A review of policy 1987–1994* London: Falmer Press.

Deakin-Crick, R. (2004) 'The Evaluating Lifelong Learning Inventory (ELLLI) Project; Final Report', University of Bristol mimeo.

Deakin-Crick, R., Broadfoot P. and Claxton, G. (2004) 'Developing and Effective Lifelong Learning Inventory' *Assessment in Education* Volume 11, Number 3, pp. 248–72.

Dearing, R. (1996) *Review of Qualifications for 16–19 year olds* (March) London: HMSO.

Department for Education and Employment/Cabinet Office (1996) 'Competitiveness: Creating the enterprise centre of europe' White Paper London: HMSO.

Department for Education and Science (1988) *National Curriculum: Task Group on Assessment and Testing – a report* London: Department for Education and Science and Welsh Office.

Department for Education and Skills (2001) *Pupil Progress in Schools: 2000 Statistics of Education* Issue number 03/01 (April).

Department for Education and Skills (2004) *Five Year Strategy for Children and Learners* CM6272 London: HMSO.

Dore, R. (1976) *The Diploma Disease* London: Allen and Unwin.

Dore, R. (1997) *The Diploma Disease* second edition London: Institute of Education.

Dweck, C. (1989) 'Motivation' in Lesgold, A. and Glazer, R. (eds) *Foundations for a Psychology of Education* Hillsdale, NJ: Earlbaum.

Earl, L. M. (2003) *Assessment as Learning* Thousand Oaks, CA: Corwin Press.

Ecclestone, K. (2002) *Learning Autonomy in Post-16 Education* London: RoutledgeFalmer.

Eckstein, M. and Noah, H. (1993) *Secondary School Examinations: International perspectives on policies and practice* Newhaven, CT: Yale University Press.

Editorial (1999) 'Exam Culture is Failing Our Students' *South China Morning Post* (5 March), p. 21.

Editorial (2002) 'Exams: You may as well flip a coin' *South China Morning Post* (6 September), p. 4.

Elliott, J. and Simons, H. (eds) (1989) *Rethinking Appraisal and Assessment* Milton Keynes: Open University Press.

Elliott, K. and Sammons, P. (2000) 'Interpreting Pupil Performance Information: Knowing your PANDA from your PICSI!' *NSIN Research Matters* (Spring/Summer), pp. 1–11.

Elwein, M. C., Glass, G. V. and Smith, M. L. (1988) 'Standards of Competence: Propositions on the nature of testing reforms' *Educational Research* (November), pp. 4–9.

Elwood, J. and Klenowski, V. (2002) 'Creating communities of shared practice: assessment use in learning and teaching', in *Journal of Assessment and Evaluation in Higher Education* Vol. 27, no. 3 pp. 243–56.

European Network of Policy Makers for the Evaluation of Education Systems (2001) *Newsletter no. 11* (December), p. 4.

Filer, A. and Pollard, A. (eds) (2000) *The Social World of Pupil Assessment in a Primary School* London: Cassell.

Firestone, W. A., Monfils, L. and Schorr, R. (2004) 'Test Preparation in New Jersey: Enquiry oriented and didactic responses' *Assessment in Education* Volume 11, Number 1 (March), pp. 49–67.

Fitzgibbon, C. (1996) *Monitoring Education: Indicators, quality and effectiveness* London: Cassell.

Foucault, M. (1977) *Discipline and Punish* London: Allen Lane.

Freedman, K. (1995) 'Assessment as Therapy: Review symposium' *Assessment in Education* Volume 2, Number 1, pp. 102–7.

Fukuyama, F. (1995) *Trust: The social virtues and the Creation of prosperity* London: Hamish Hamilton.

Gardner, H. (1999) *Intelligence Reframed: Multiple intelligences for the 21st century* New York: Basic Books.

Gardner, J. and Cowan, P. (2005) 'The Fallibility of High Stakes "11-plus" Testing in Northern Ireland' *Assessment in Education* Volume 12, Number 2, pp. 145–65.

Gauthier, P. (ed.) (2004) 'L'Examen: Lieu de l'équité scolaire?' *Revue International d'Education* 37 (Decembre), pp. 23–9.

Gipps, C. (1995) *Beyond Testing: Towards a theory of educational assessment* London: Routledge/Falmer.

Goldstein, H. (2002) 'International Comparative Assessment: How far have we really come? *Assessment in Education* Volume 11, Number 2, pp. 227–35.

Goldstein, H. and Sutherland, G. (eds) (2001) 'Assessment at the Millennium' *Assessment in Education* Volume 8, Number 1 (March).

Goleman, D. (1996) *Emotional Intelligence* London: Bloomsbury.

Goleman, D. (1999) *Working with Emotional Intelligence* London: Bantham Books.

Gonczi A. (1994) 'Competency-based assessment in the professions in Australia' in *Assessment in Education* Vol. II no. 1, pp. 27–45.

Halpin, D., Marny, D., Power, S., Whitty, G. and Gewirtz, S. (2004) 'Curriculum Innovation Within an Evaluative State: Issues of risk and regulation' *The Curriculum Journal* Volume 5, Number 3, pp. 197–207.

Halsall, R. (2001) 'School Improvement: The need for vision and reprofessionalisation' *British Educational Research Journal* Volume 27, Number 4, pp. 505–9.

Hargreaves, D. (1992) *Report of the Committee on the Curriculum and Organisation of ILEA Secondary Schools* London: ILEA.

Hargreaves, D. (2004) *Learning for Life: The foundations of lifelong learning* Bristol: The Policy Press.

Harland, J. (1986) 'An evaluation catechism' University of London Institute of Education, mimeo.

Harlen, W. (ed.) (1994) *Enhancing Quality in Assessment* London: Paul Chapman.

Harlen, W. and Deakin-Crick, R. (2002) *Testing Motivation and Learning* Cambridge: Assessment Reform Group Cambridge University School of Education.

Harlen, W. and Deakin-Crick, R. (2003) 'The Impact of Summative Assessment on Students' Motivation for Learning' *Assessment in Education* Volume 10, Number 1.

Harlen, W. and Elliott, J. (1982) 'A Checklist for Planning or Reviewing Evaluation' in McCormick, R., Bynner, J., Clift, P., James, M. and Morrow Brown, C. (1982) *Calling Education to Account* Buckingham: Heinemann/Open University Press.

Harlen, W. and James, M. (1997) 'Assessment and Learning: Differences and relationships between formative and summative assessment' *Assessment in Education* Volume 4, Number 3, pp. 365–79.

Harthog, P. and Rhodes, E. C. (1935) *An Examination of Examinations* London: Macmillan.

Hartley, L. and Broadfoot, P. (1986) 'Assessing Teacher Performance' *Journal of Education Policy* Volume 3, Number 1, pp. 39–45.

Harvey, L. and Green, D. (1993) 'Defining quality' in *Assessment and Evaluation in Higher Education*, Vol. 18 no. 1, pp. 9–15

Hill, P. (2004) 'Take Cardinal Newman Approach, Lecturers Told' *Times Higher Education Supplement* (10 September), p. 11.

Hinett, K. (1995) 'Fighting the Assessment War: The idea of assessment-in-learning' *Quality in Higher Education* Volume 1, Number 3, pp. 211–22.

Hinett, K. and Thomas, J. (eds) (1999) *Staff Guide to Self and Peer Assessment for the Self-Assessment in Professional and Higher Education (SAPHE) Project* Oxford: OCLSD.

Hiscock, D. (2004) 'I'm Sorry I Nodded Off': Exam fears driving teenagers to Prozac' *The Guardian* (15 June).

HMI (1985) *Quality in Schools: Evaluation and appraisal* London: HMSO.

Hopes, C. (1997) *Assessing, Evaluating and Assuring Quality in Schools in the European Union* Frankfurt: Deutsches Institut für Internationale Padogogische Forschung.

House, E. (ed.) (1986) *New Directions in Educational Evaluation* London: Falmer Press.

Hufton, N., Elliot, J. and Illushin, L. (2006) 'Teachers' Beliefs About Student Motivation: Similarities and differences across cultures' *Comparative Education*.

Hughes, P. (1998) *Appraisal in UK Higher Education* Sheffield: Universities and Colleges Staff Development Agency.

Hursh, D. (2005) 'The Growth of High-Stakes Testing in the USA: Accountability, markets and the decline in educational equality' Br Ed Res J vol 31 no 5 pp. 605–22.

Ingenkamp, K. (1977) *Educational Assessment* Windsor: NFER.

Jackson, N. (2001) 'Personal Development Planning: What does it mean?' PDP Working Paper 1, Version 4 (June), York: LTSN.

James, M. (1998) *Using Assessment for School Improvement* London: Heinemann.

James, M. (2000) 'Measured Lives: The rise of assessment as the engine of change in English schools' *The Curriculum Journal* Volume 11, Number 3, pp. 343–64.

James, M. and Brown, S. (2005) 'Grasping the TLRP Nettle: Preliminary analysis and some enduring issues surrounding the improvement of learning outcomes' *The Curriculum Journal* Volume 16, Number 1 (March), pp. 7–30.

Johnson, P. (1991) 'Re-Thinking Assessment' *Language Matters* CLPE, Number 2, p. 7.

Karsten, S. and Visscher, A. (2001) 'Publishing School Performance Indicators' *Prospects* Volume X, Number 2 (June), pp. 239–53.

Kellaghan, T. and Greaney, V. (2001) 'The Globalisation of Assessment in the Twentieth Century' *Assessment in Education* Volume 8, pp. 87–102.

Kincheloe, J. E., Steinberg, S. R. and Gresson, A. D. (1996) *Measured Lies: The bell curve examined* New York: St Martin's Griffin.

Kite, M. (2002) 'Labour Misses 75% of Targets Tied to Funding' *The Times* (18 November), p. 2.

Klenowski, V. (2002) *Developing Portfolios for Learning and Assessment* London: RoutledgeFalmer.

Ko, E. (2001) 'Performance appraisal in higher education: the impact of new managerialism an academic staff' Ed. Dip Thesis, University of Bristol.

Kogan, M. (1986) *Educational Accountability* London: Hutchinson.

Koretz, D., Broadfoot, P. and Wolf, A. (eds) (1998) 'Portfolios and Records of Achievement' *Assessment in Education* special issue, Volume 5, Number 3 (November), pp. 301–481.

Lave, J. and Wenger, E. (1991) *Situated Learning: Legitimate peripheral participation* Cambridge: Cambridge University Press.

Lee-Smith, M. (1990) *The Role of Testing in Elementary Schools* SCE Technical Report 321, Los Angeles, CA: Arizona State University, pp. 521–42.

Lee-Smith, M. (1991) 'Meaning of Test Preparation' *American Educational Research Journal* Volume 28, Number 3.

Leitch, S. (2005) 'Skills in the UK: The Long-Term Challenge' Interim Report of the Leitch Review of Skills London: HMSO.

Lewin, K. (1997) *Assessment in Education*, pp. 137–61.

Little, A. (ed.) (1997) 'The Diploma Disease Twenty Years On' *Assessment in Education* Volume 4, Number 1 (January).

Little, A. (2000) 'Globalization, qualifications and livelihoods: towards a research agenda' *Assessment in Education*

Livingstone, Sir Richard (1941) *Education for a World Adrift* Oxford: Oxford University Press.

Lucas, W. (1999) 'Destination Everywhere' *Times Educational Supplement* (9 January), p. 19.

MacDonald, B. (1974) 'Evaluation and the Control of Education' reprinted in Murphy, R. and Torrance, H. (eds) *Evaluating Education* London: Harper and Row.

McFarlane, A. E. (ed.) (2003) 'Assessment for the Digital Age', *Assessment in Education* Volume 10, Number 3.

McGettrick, B. (2002) personal communication.

McGuiness, C. (1999) *From Thinking Schools to Thinking Classrooms: A review and evaluation of approaches for developing pupils' thinking* DfEE Research Report 115.

McGuinness, M. (2002) 'McGuinness Announces Transfer Tests Are to Go' press release (8 October) Bangor, NI: Department of Education.

Mackintosh, H. (1994) *A Comparative Study of Current Theories and Practices in Assessing Students' Achievements at Primary and Secondary Level Final report* IBE Document Series No. 4 (April) Geneva: IBE.

Maclintosh, H. G. and Hale, D. E. (1976) *Assessment and the Secondary School Teacher* London: RKP.

McMeniman, M. (1989) 'Motivation to Learn' in Langford, P. (ed.) *Educational Psychology: An Australian perspective* Longman.

Madaus, G. (1991) 'The Effects of Important Tests on Students: Implications for a national examination or system of examinations' paper, American Educational Research Association Invitational Conference on Accountability as a State Reform Instrument Washington DC (June).

Madaus, G. (1993) 'A National Testing System: Manna from above? An historical/technological perspective' *Educational Assessment* Volume 1, Number 1, pp. 9–26.

Madaus, G. and Clark, M. (2001) *The adverse impact of high-stakes testing on British students*: evidence from 100 years of test data.

Madaus, G. and Kellaghan, T. (1991) *Student Examination Systems in the EC: Lessons for the United States Office of Technology Assessment* Washington: US Congress.

Mahoney, P., Menter, I. and Hextall, I. (2004) 'The Emotional Impact of Performance-Related Pay on Teachers in England' *British Educational Research Journal* Volume 30, Number 3, pp. 435–57.

Massey, A., Green, S., Dexter, T. and Hamnet, L. (2003) 'Comparability of National Tests Over Time: Key Stage I, Key Stage II and Key Stage III standards between 1996 and 2001' *Final Report to QCA of the Comparability Over Time Project* Cambridge: UCLES.

Menter, I., Mahoney, P. and Hextall, I. (2004) 'Ne'er the Twain Shall Meet? Modernising the teaching profession in Scotland and England' *Journal of Education Policy* Volume 19, pp. 195–214.

Merrett, J. and Merrett, F. (1992) 'Classroom Management for Project Work: An application of correspondence training' *Educational Studies* Volume 18.

Messick, S. (1995) 'Validity of Psychological Assessment' *American Psychologist* Volume 50, Number 9, pp. 741–9.

Ministère de L'éducation nationale (2006) *L'Etat de L'école de la maternelle a l'enseignement superieur: 30 indicateurs sur le system educatif francais* Number 16 (Octobre) Paris: DEPP.

Mislevy, R. J., Yamamoto, K. and Anacker, S. (1991) *Towards a Test Theory for Assessing Student Understanding* ETS Princeton Research Report.

Mortimore, J. and Mortimore, P. (1984) 'Secondary School Examinations: Helpful servant or dominating masters?' *Bedford Way Papers* Number 18, London Institute of Education.

Mortimore, P., Sammons, P., Stoll, L., Lewis, D. and Ecob, R. (1998) *School Matters* Wells: Open Books.

Moser, C. (1999) 'What Motivates People to Learn?' Goodison Group Seminar, London (9 September).

Moskowitz, J. H. and Stevens, M. (2004) *Comparing Learning Outcomes: International assessment and education policy* London: RoutledgeFalmer.

Muller (1977) cited in Frey, J (1992) *History and Future of Qualifications* paper, Qualifications for the 21st Century Conference New Zealand Qualifications Association.

Munns, G. and Woodward, H. (2004) 'Insiders' Voices: Self-assessment and student engagement' EARLI conference, Bergen, Norway.

Murphy, R. and Broadfoot, P. (eds) (1995) *Effective Assessment and the Improvement of Education* London: Falmer Press.

Murphy, R. and Torrance, H. (eds) (1987) *Evaluating Education: Issues and methods* London: Harper and Row.

Naismith, D. (1990) 'Effectiveness and Evaluation in Educational Institutions' in Entwistle, N. (ed.) *Handbook of Educational Ideas and Practices* London: Routledge.

Natriello, G. (1987) 'The Impact of Evaluation Processes on Students' *Educational Psycholgist* Volume 22, Number 2, pp. 155–75.

Neave, G. (1989) 'On the Cultivation of Quality, Efficiency and Enterprise: An overview of recent trends in higher education in Western Europe' *European Journal of Education* Volume 19, Number 2, pp. 111–29.

Newton, P. (2005) 'The Public Understanding of Measurement Inaccuracy' *British Educational Research Journal* Volume 31, Number 4, pp. 419–42.

Noah, H. and Eckstein, M. (1990) 'Trade-offs in Examination Policies: An international comparative perspective' in Broadfoot, P. et al. *Changing Educational Assessment* London: Routledge.

Nuttall, D. L. (1987) 'The Validity of Assessments' *European Journal of Psychology of Education* Volume 11, Number 2, pp. 109–18.

Nuttall, D. L. (1994) 'Choosing Indicators' in Riley, K. and Nuttall, D. L. (eds) *Measuring Quality: Education indicators – United Kingdom and international perspectives* London: Falmer Press.

Ochert, A. (1999) 'A Time and Emotion Study' *Times Higher Education Supplement* (4 June), pp. 20–1.

OECD (2006) *Education at a Glance* Paris: OECD. www.oecd.org/document/52/0,2340,en_2649_201185_37328564_1_1_1_1,00.html

OECD/PISA (2003) *Programme for International Student Assessment* Paris: OECD.

O'Neill, O. (2002) 'A Question of Trust' The Reith Lectures, Cambridge: Cambridge University Press.

Orfield, G. and Kornharber, M. (eds) *Raising Standards or Raising Barriers? Inequality and high-stakes testing in public education*. New York: The Century Foundation.

Osborn, M., Broadfoot, P., McNess, E., Planel, C., Ravn, B. and Triggs, P. (2003) *A World of Difference? Comparing learners across europe* Maidenhead: Open University Press.

PA Consulting (2004) *Better Accountability Revisited: Review of accountability costs* Bristol: Higher Education Funding Council.

Parlett, M. and Hamilton, D. (1976) 'Evaluation as Illumination' in Tawney, D. (ed.) *Curriculum Evaluation Today* London: Macmillan.

Perkins, D. (1995) *Outsmarting IQ*: *The emerging science of learnable intelligence* New York, NY: The Free Press.

Perrenoud, P. (1989) in Western, P. (ed.) (1991) *Assessment of Pupil Achievement and Schools' Success* Brussels: Swets and Zeitlinger.

Pidgeon, D. and Yates, A. (1968) *An Introduction to Educational Measurement* London: RKP.

PISA *Measuring Student Knowledge and Skills: A new framework for assessment* Paris: PISA OECD. www.pisa. oecd.org

Pitman, J. (2003) 'What Young People Say: Messages for educators' International Association for Educational Assessment Annual Conference, Manchester, UK.

Pollard, A., Broadfoot, P., Croll, P., Osborn, M. and Abbott, D. (1994) *Changing English Primary Schools? The impact of the Education Reform Act at Key Stage One* London: Cassell.

Pollard, A., Triggs, P. with Broadfoot, P. and McNess, E. (2000) *What Pupils Say: Changing policy and practice in primary education* London: Cassell.

Porter, A. and Gamoran, A. (eds) (2002) *Review of Methodological Advances in Cross-Nation Surveys of Educational Achievement* Washington, DC: National Academy Press.

Powell, L. A. (2000) 'Realising the Value of Self-Assessment: The influence of the business model on teacher professionalism' *European Journal of Teacher Education* Volume 23, Number 1, pp. 37–48.

Power, M. (1997) 'The Audit Society: Rituals of verification' *Quality in Higher Education* Volume 1, pp. 211–22.

Prensky, M. (2001) *On the Horizon* NCB University Press, Volume 9, Number 5 (October)

Prensky, M. (2003) *Beyond the Exam: Innovative approaches to learning and assessment* Bristol: Futurelab.

Quicke, J. and Winter, C. (1994) 'Teaching the Language of Learning: Towards a meta-cognitive approach to pupil empowerment' *British Educational Research Journal* Volume 20, pp. 429–45.

Reineke, R. (1998) *Challenging the Mind, Touching the Heart: Best assessment practices* Thousand Oaks, CA: Corwin Press.

Ridgway, J. (2004) *What Technology Can and Cannot Do for Assessment: Beyond the exam* Bristol: Futurelab.

Roan, M. (2003) 'Changes in Marking UK Examinations: Are we ready yet?' International Association for Educational Achievement Annual Conference, Manchester, UK.

Robinson, P. (1999) 'The Tyranny of League Tables: International comparisons of educational attainment and economic performance' in Alexander, R., Broadfoot, P. and Phillips, D. (eds) *Learning from Comparing Vol. 1* Oxford: Symposium Books, pp. 217–37.

Roderick, M. and Engel, M. (2001) 'The Grasshopper and the Ant: Motivational responses of low-achieving students to high-stakes testing *Educational Evaluation and Policy Analysis* Volume 23, Number 3 (Fall), pp. 197–227.

Roos, B. and Hamilton, D. (2005) 'Formative Assessment: A cybernetic viewpoint' *Assessment in Education* Volume 12, Number 1 (March), pp. 7–20.

Ross, M. (ed.) (1986) *Assessment in Arts Education: A necessary discipline or a loss of happiness?* London: Pergamon Press.

Russell, J. (2005) 'Yes They Get Good Results But by God Are They Bored' *The Guardian* (26 August), p. 28.

Ryan, A. (2005) 'The QAA Is Obviously Adopting a Policy of "Reculer Pour Mieux Sauter" and Abandoning Subject Reviews to Preserve the Rest of its Operations' *Times Higher Education Supplement* (12 August), p. 13.

Ryan, A. and Patrick, H. (2001) 'The Classroom Social Environment and Changes in Adolescents' Motivation and Engagement During Middle School' *American Educational Research Journal* Volume 38, p. 2.

Sacks, P. (1999) *Standardized Minds: The high price of America's testing culture and what we can do to change it* Cambridge, MA: Perseus Books.

Sadler, D. R. (1989) 'Formative Assessment and the Design of Instructional Systems' *Instructional Science* Volume 18, pp. 119–44.

Satterly, D. (1992) *Assessment in Schools* Oxford: Blackwell.

Shepard, L. A. (2000) 'The Role of Assessment in a Learning Culture' *Educational Researcher* (February), p. 14.

Standaert, R. (2001) *Inspectorates of Education in Europe* Leuven, Belgium: Acco.

Steinberg, R. (1996) *Beyond the Classroom: Why school reform has failed and what parents need to do* New York, NY: Touchstone.

Stenhouse, L. (1979) 'Case Study in Comparative Education: Particularity and Generalisation' *Comparative Education* Volume 15, Number 1 (March), pp. 5–10.

Sternberg, R. J. 'Myths, Countermyths and Truths About Intelligence' *Educational Researcher* pp. 11–16.

Stevenson, R. J. and Palmer, J. A. (1994) *Learning: Principles, processes and practices* London: Cassell.

Stiggins, R. (2004) 'New Assessment Beliefs for a New School Mission' *Phi Delta Kappan* (September), pp. 22–7.

Strathern, M. (2000) 'The Tyranny of Transparency' *British Educational Research Journal* Volume 26, Number 3, pp. 309–21.

Sutton, R. (2000) *Assessment for Learning* RS Publications.

Tharpe, R. G. and Gallimore, R. (1988) *Rousing Minds to Life: Teaching learning and schooling in social context* Cambridge: Cambridge University Press.

The Guardian (2005) 'The Guardian's Top Schools' (25 August), p. 9.

Tomlinson, J. (1992) 'Retrospect on Ruskin: Prospect on the 1990s' University of Warwick, mimeo.

Tomlinson, M. (2004) Presentation to Russell Group, Swindon.

Tomlinson Report (2004) *Curriculum and Qualifications Reform: The Final Report of the Working Group on 14–19 DFES 0796* London: HMSO.

Torrance, H. (2002) 'Can Testing Really Raise Educational Standards?' Inaugural lecture, University of Sussex, mimeo.

Torrance, H. and Coultas, J. (2004) *Do Summative Assessment and Testing Have a Positive Effect on Post-16 Learners? Motivation for earning in the learning and skills sector – a review of the research literature on assessment in post-compulsory education in the UK* London: Learning and Skills Research Centre.

Townsend, M. (2004) 'Teenage Suicide' *The Observer* (6 June).

Troman, G. (2000) 'Teacher Stress in the Low Trust Society' *British Journal of Sociology of Education* Volume 21, Number 3, pp. 331–55.

Tymms, P. (2004) 'Are Standards Rising in English Primary Schools?' *British Educational Research Journal* Volume 30, Number 4, pp. 477–94.

US National Council on Educational Standards and Testing (1992) cited in Madaus, G. and Kellaghan, T. (1991) *Student Examination Systems in the EC: Lessons for the United States* Washington, DC: Office of Technology Assessment, US Congress, p. 23.

Vinokur, A. (ed.) (2005) 'Pouviers et mesure en éducation' Association pour la recherché sur l'education et les savoirs hors-serie no 1 (Juin), Paris.

Vygotsky, L. (1978) *Mind in Society* Cambridge, MA: MIT Press.

Watkins, C. with Carnell, E., Lodge, C., Wagner, P. and Whalley, C. (2001) 'Learning About Learning Enhances Performance' *NSIN Research Matters* 13.

Weeden, P., Winter, J. and Broadfoot, P. (2002) *Assessment: What's in It for Schools?* London: RoutledgeFalmer.

Wheeler, B., Shaw, M., Mitchell, R. and Dorling, D. (2005) 'Using Millennial Census Data to Understand Poverty, Inequality and Place' *Life in Britain* Bristol: The Policy Press.

Wiliam, D. and Blee, C. (2001) 'Teachers Developing Assessment for Learning: Impact on student achievement' British Educational Research Association Annual Conference, Leeds.

Wiliam, D., Lee, C., Harrison, C. and Black, P. (2004) 'Teachers Developing Assessment for Learning: Impact on Student Achievement' *Assessment in Education* Volume 11, Number 1, pp. 49–67.

Wilson, D., Croxson, B. and Atkinson, A. (2005) 'School Performance: How head teachers respond to measurement' *Market and Public Organisation* Number 12 (Winter), Bristol: CMPO.

Wolf, A. (2002) *Does Education Matter? Myths about education and economic growth* London: Penguin.

Wolf, A. and Bakker, S. (2001) *Assessment Journal*

Wragg, T., Wikeley, F., Wragg, C. and Haynes, G. (1996) *Teacher Appraisal Observed* London: Routledge.

Glossary

A-learning
Individualized, information technology – facilitated formative feedback.

Accreditation
Formal qualification given for a specified achievement.

Affective domain
Relating to feelings, emotions and attitudes.

Appraisal
A general review of performance.

Assessment for learning
Assessment oriented to feedback and motivation for students in order to support learning rather than to judge or measure it.

Assessment literacy
Knowledge and understanding of the effective use of assessment in relation to particular purposes.

Authentic assessment
Approaches to assessment that seek to model as closely as possible the real-life application of the skills or knowledge it is desired to judge.

Categoric assessment
An approach to assessment in which a student's level of performance is described in terms of specified levels of achievement.

Certification
The recognition of a particular level of achievement or defined quality of performance through the provision of a certificate.

Cognitive domain
Pertaining to intellectual operations such as remembering, reasoning, analysing and understanding.

Communities of practice
A group of individuals engaged in a collective task or activity.

Consequential validity
The impact that a particular test or assessment has on the priorities and practices of the population in which it is administered.

Criterion-referenced
Assessment that is designed to provide a pass/fail decision in relation to a defined standard.

Diagnostic assessment
Assessment that is designed to identify a student's strengths and weaknesses in relation to a given learning task.

E-assessment
Assessment that is conducted using a computer interface.

E-learning
Learning that is facilitated and supported through computer–student interaction.

Evaluative assessment
A term often used to refer to the assessment of institutions and systems rather than individuals.

Extrinsic motivation
The effort expended in order to reach a particular goal in the hope of achieving a desired reward.

Feedback
Information provided to the learner concerning the strengths and weaknesses of a particular performance.

Formative assessment
Assessment that is designed to support and guide the learning process.

High-stakes assessment
Assessment that has important consequences for individuals or institutions.

Intrinsic motivation
The effort expended on a task that derives from enjoyment and satisfaction in the task itself.

Learning power
The combination of attitudes and skills that shape the nature and level of an individual's engagement in a subject or task at any particular time.

Locus of control
The degree to which an individual is inclined to take personal responsibility for particular goals or outcomes.

Meta-learning
Learning about learning – awareness of the process and elements of learning.

Metacognitive skill
The capacity to monitor one's own strengths and weaknesses in relation to a particular task or desired goal.

Norm-referenced
Assessment that is designed to provide a spread of candidates' test scores in order to rank them.

Performance-based assessment
Often used as an alternative to 'authentic assessment' where the aim is to capture as much of the quality of a 'real-life' performance as possible.

Performativity
A focus on maximizing test scores for individuals or institutions.

Portfolio
A collection of work or records of different kinds that is designed to provide evidence of achievements and skills.

Psychometrics
The pursuit of techniques designed to provide objective measures of an individual's innate intellectual ability.

Record of achievement
A summative portfolio of evidence concerning qualifications, experience and skills typically provided at the end of a particular stage of study.

Reliability
The dependability of a particular assessment or test instrument as measured, for example, by its capacity to produce the same result when used on another occasion.

Selection
The use of assessment as the basis for choosing some individuals out of a larger group.

Self-assessment
A formative or summative assessment of performance or quality that is conducted by an individual or an institution of itself.

Summative assessment
Assessment that is carried out at the end of a particular course of learning or educational stage that describes the level of achievement reached.

Validity
The extent to which any particular test or assessment faithfully reflects the level of achievement or skill that it is designed to measure.

Washback effect
The impact of the existence of a particular assessment on the learning priorities of individuals or institutions.

Zone of Proximal Development (ZPD)
A term coined by the Russian psychologist Vygotsky to describe the appropriate next steps in an individual's learning.

Index